POLITICAL THEORY:
ITS NATURE AND USES

St. Martin's Series

in American Politics

POLITICAL
THEORY
Its Nature
and Uses

GEORGE KATEB
Amherst College

ST. MARTIN'S PRESS · NEW YORK

To my sisters—Jeanette, Elaine and Judith

Preface

There are many ways to study political theory. In this essay, I have suggested some of the questions political theorists have traditionally asked, and the sorts of answers they have given. I have also tried to show that recurrent as the questions are, and powerful as the answers are, much of the richness of political theory comes out in the course of asking the questions and giving the answers. We must resist the temptation to treat a political theory as if it were a catechism. In addition, I have tried to indicate some of the reasons for esteeming political theory. Such an apologetic task was not always necessary; but it is now, because there are many students of politics who feel that their profession has outgrown the dead masters, and that political science, for the most part, begins in the twentieth century.

My approach is not chronological, and it is very selective. I do not cite all those who qualify for the title of political theorist: the names of Hume and James Mill, for example, do not appear in the body of the text. I have not often mentioned the ancillary writings of political theorists, valuable though they are. I have not referred to the changes of mind many political theorists underwent. Rather, I have directed attention, admittedly unevenly, to a few political theorists and to the books for which they are largely famous. My aim is not to cover a vast field, but (to put it incautiously) to impose a pattern on a series of works, most of them works of genius.

I wish to express my appreciation to Earl Latham for his careful reading of the manuscript, and for the many incisive and helpful comments he made.

I would also like to thank Mrs. James Crosson for her skill and patience as a typist.

Contents

Chapter I

THE MAIN CHARACTERISTICS
OF POLITICAL THEORY

By tradition, the phrase "political theory" refers to those writings which deal with politics from a broadly moral point of view. For undergraduates and graduate students alike, courses in political theory mean readings in the "classical texts" or "great books" of politics—books that are most of them old, all engaged in some moral pursuit or other, and almost all betraying some connection to large human concerns. We should acknowledge, however, that though this is the traditional way of using the phrase, "political theory" has been and can be used, quite properly, to name other kinds of intellectual endeavor. For instance, David Easton, in his very influential book *The Political System*, distinguishes between *value* theory and *causal* theory. The former is what we usually think of as political theory. The latter is theory in the scientific sense of the word. Thus, causal theory would be the body of laws or generalizations, established by scientific technique and with scientific rigor, concerning political activity. Causal theory "seeks to show the relation among political facts."[1] As Easton demonstrates, value theory and causal theory rarely if ever

[1] David Easton, *The Political System* (New York: Alfred A. Knopf, 1953), p. 52.

exist apart from each other: they not only need each other, but are inextricably intertwined. Political scientists studying political activity are, after all, human beings studying the activity of other human beings. The values of the observer affect his choice of what to study and what he sees when he studies, while the objects of his study are creatures possessed of values and engaged in purposive behavior which, to be understood fully, must be understood imaginatively.

The First Essential Characteristic: Moral

Nevertheless, it is still possible to separate traditional political theory from causal or scientific political theory. The distinction is based on ultimate intention. All the writers read in political theory courses are, first and last, moral in their interest in (often obsession with) politics. They seek to persuade, convince, or convert others to a political attitude or undertaking. Many aim to reform political life; a few to remake it altogether. Their intellectual and rhetorical resources are summoned and employed with the hope of changing—sometimes saving—the world, or at least part of it. The causal theorist, the political scientist, on the other hand, is primarily interested in accumulating or refining political knowledge, without any necessary or intimate moral ambition. Whatever the degree of his success at being scientific—that is, objective, impartial, free of prejudice—his aim is to be scientific. He will almost certainly have moral views, historical sympathies, policy preferences; but he will try to prevent their interfering with his observations and interpretations. He is devoted to the truth despite the pain it may sometimes cost him to tell it.

If therefore we try to characterize political theory, we must begin by saying that values sit at its center. Sometimes appearances may be to the contrary. Machiavelli's *The Prince* seems to be wholly a book promiscuously teaching the techniques of power to any interested reader—until we come to its last pages which burn with a passion for the salvation of Italy. The sincerity or congruence of these pages has been questioned many times; even without them, however, a moral sense, at the minimum, is flickeringly present throughout Machiavelli's little handbook. He hates villains, those gratuitously cruel, as much as he admires those who are manly in political affairs. And continuously present is the awareness of the unsuitability of the Christian conscience for guiding men in either the means or ends of politics. Again, Hobbes's pretense is that he is an observer helpless in the face of what he wishes to describe. He will not lament human nature or impute sin to men; he will faithfully record the necessities to which men are subject; he will simply draw the inevitable conclusions from the facts of nature. Yet everywhere in the *Leviathan*, judgments are made, practices are advocated, possibilities are canvassed; there is mockery and despair.

To make the point general: all the books, fragments, or essays included within the corpus of political theory have a moral purpose, despite the disguises and self-deceptions of a given political theorist. The question that unifies any political theory is, What ends or purposes *should* government serve?

The Second Essential Characteristic: Inclusive

Three other qualities are shared by all the writing commonly considered as political theory. There is first the quality of being inclusive. Political theorists are interested in whole systems of politics. Though they may turn their attention to specific moral dilemmas and to matters of detailed political practice, their ambition extends beyond that. They are not content with being partial, though they may be remembered chiefly for certain points, solutions, or suggestions. Their work seeks to provide the lineaments of a complete doctrine of government. Recommendations dealing with the major features of political life are composed into one large scheme for practice, one full answer to the question, Given certain ends or purposes that government should serve, what must government be if it is to serve those ends or purposes? How must it be organized, what powers should it have, what functions should it take on itself, what limits should it respect, who may qualify to rule or to judge or to bear arms or to vote? Naturally, there are differences of emphasis and selectivity from theorist to theorist.

The Third Essential Characteristic: Philosophical

There is next the quality of being philosophical. Political theory is sometimes called "political philosophy." This name points unmistakably to the fact that political theorists are engaged in an enterprise in which obvious facts are pondered and elementary questions are asked, in which many things that the world takes for granted, or takes as settled, are subjected to close scrutiny. The answers given by political theorists, the conclusions they reach, are not necessarily critical, radical, or novel. Sometimes, as in the case of conservative political theorists, the political world, as it exists, is left intact, with nothing more given to it than better reasons than it customarily uses for defending itself—although there is doubtless something disturbing in the very act of talking seriously about an established institution. To the timid, to those who want the *status quo* regarded as sacrosanct, even praise may appear as a sign of apology. And to some degree, this fear is justified: the conservative political theorist, because he is a political theorist, never stays completely within the confines of common opinion. He stirs up trouble by inviting response. In any case, the political theorist tries to go back to the sources of political life in human necessities, tries to identify or define the first principles that ought to govern political discourse, tries to locate the political sector of life in relation to the other sectors of life. He is a theorist precisely because he believes that much has to be said, many connections have to be made, many difficulties faced, if his answer is to be convincing and make its way in competition with other answers. A writer conventionally accorded the title of political theorist does not go straight to his answers: by the time he finishes, he will have made an image of man and imparted an entire sense of politics. Whatever his final views, he begins with the assumption that politics is problematic, that its means are morally dubious and its ends morally preemptive, that the subject of politics is supremely important because politics involves men in a sizable or important portion of the totality of their moral relations. It should be made clear that when we speak of the philosophical habit of mind, we do not mean to suggest that each political theorist derives his political theory from an all-embracing metaphysical system—some do, some do not; or that each aspires to an all-embracing metaphysical system and looks upon his political theory as a necessary contribution to the completion of that system—again, some do, some do not. In this context, "philosophy" means a manner of intellectual procedure, and nothing more.

The Fourth Essential Characteristic: General

There is last the quality of being general. Some political theorists intend their work to achieve specific results in the world around them in the present or near future; some political theorists are more detached, less urgent in their wish to make things happen in the real world and make them happen immediately. Whatever the case, however, the political theorist does not let the problems facing him and his society exhaust his interest, even though those problems wear the aspect of emergency. The writers address themselves to others than their contemporaries; they are absorbed by politics in itself, not just the politics of their time and place; and the considerations they adduce, the arguments they make, the concepts they use, the learning they lean on, and the learning they wish to convey are all, if not timeless, then meant to endure. More particularly, their writings are meant to be *useful* to future generations, not merely to endure as curiosities or ingenious structures of thought.

In short, when we look over the succession of political theories—from Plato's *Republic* and Aristotle's *Politics* and Cicero's *Laws* to Marsilius's *The Defender of Peace* and Bodin's *Six Books of the Commonwealth* and Machiavelli's *The Prince* and Hobbes's *Leviathan* to Locke's *Two Treatises of Civil Government* and Rousseau's *The Social Contract* and Hegel's *Philosophy of Right* and Mill's *On Liberty* (combined with his *Considerations on Representative Government*)—we see that what unites these books, what defines political theory is an approach to political life that is moral (or normative) in intent, inclusive in scope, philosophical in procedure, and general in relevance. It would seem impossible to find anything else of significance (except their high quality) that does unite these writings.

Other Characteristics That May Be Present

We must next point to a feature present in many works of political theory, though not in some of the greatest. That is formality, which can mean orderliness of presentation, or scrupulous attention to the construction and consistency of argument, or both. Which is to say that a political theory is frequently systematic, in the same way in which a work of metaphysics is systematic. Hobbes's *Leviathan* and Hegel's *Philosophy of Right* are manifestly and proudly systematic, and simply for being so can compel either profound admiration or profound distaste. At the other extreme is a book like Burke's *Reflections on the Revolution in France,* which is lacking almost totally in formality or system. Yet the opposite of systematic is not slovenly. Burke shows the same capacity to think strenuously, to think philosophically, about issues of the greatest toughness and importance, while allowing his argument to unfold almost casually, in the form of a letter. He pays little attention to the clarification of concepts; he constructs no architecture of ideas. His tone is that of a man of the world confronting men of the world. For all that, the result is one of the main texts in the history of political theory, a book born from the pressure of momentous events, but rising above events, rising above Burke's panic, to formulate a moral view of politics—a conservative political theory—that no other conservative has ever bettered.

Between the extremes of Burke and Hobbes, there are, of course, numerous intermediary styles. Thus Locke's *Second Treatise* is generally thought to be less systematic, less disciplined in its composition, than Hobbes's *Leviathan.* Locke repeats himself, goes through the motions of illustrating his assertions now and then, alters his treatment of the same subject in different parts of the book, and is sometimes careless in his use of key words (like "property"). But it is clear, if only from his chapter headings, that Locke intended his treatise to develop step by step, the main divisions of his subject to be taken up one by one in a sensible order. That Locke only partly succeeded in the task he set for himself should be acknowledged; but once that is acknowledged, the comparative unimportance of being systematic is actually disclosed. The cumulative richness of Locke's text finally silences—or should silence—disparagement of his capacities to reason about politics. Difficulties of many sorts remain for those who would understand Locke's theory. These are the difficulties, however, that come from following the attempt of an extraordinary mind to impose order on, to make sense of, complex phenomena, phenomena that resist simple treatment and keep breaking out of the confines of even the most careful theory. Our conclusion must be that the presence of system in a political theory is not, by itself, a sign of the excellence (or lack of excellence) of that theory, and that the failure of a systematic approach to be thoroughly systematic is no indication—or a minor indication, at best—of the quality of a political theory.

As political theorists vary on the matter of system, they also differ in the degree to which they are occupied by questions that are not strictly political, but rather politically pertinent—specifically, psychological and sociological questions. The distinction between psychological and socio-logical is largely artificial. Society is made up of the activity of human beings; the activity of human beings is mostly carried on according to the rules, forms, and patterns given by society. The social and the psycho-logical blend into one. However, there are certain times when analysis is served by separating what in practice is not separable, by viewing the same thing from different angles. We make the distinction here in order to point to two main kinds of inquiry often found in works of political theory.

The first, the psychological, pertains to the effort made by most political theorists to come to an understanding of human nature. At first sight, there would seem to be something hopeless about such an en-deavor. Who, after all, is capable of mastering the inconceivable diversity of human experience and the treacherous elusiveness of human motiva-tion? What one mind can possibly be strong enough to assimilate and arrange all that must be known if human nature is to be known? To leave aside the question of whether it is even proper to speak of human nature in the abstract and without reference to particular cultures and historical periods, does it seem likely that human nature is a fit subject for brief and amateur discourse?

The second, the sociological, pertains to the effort made by a few political theorists to come to an understanding of social institutions in the totality of their workings. Again, such an effort must appear to be presumptuous. If the human mind is complicated beyond description, cannot the same be said of the network of "interpersonal" relationships? If abstract psychology is open to the charge of being inevitably reductive of the richness of the human mind, is not general sociology open to the charge of failing to appreciate both the vastness and the intricacy of any society?

It may be that theorizing about government is a defensible intellec-tual operation, but do "man" and "society" lend themselves to this treat-ment? The answer is that unless allowance is made, the psychological and sociological content of the various political theories will doubtless be thought inadequate, or even contemptible. No single writer has ever "explained" man or society, despite the sometimes incredible confidence displayed in the effort to do so. It may as well be admitted that modesty is not characteristic of political theorists. Hobbes disposes of Man in sixteen chapters of *Leviathan;* in a hundred pages, Rousseau describes the origin of human inequality. But their arrogance also has its limits. They are not literally aiming at perfect and complete knowledge, whatever that may be. Their interest is in fact quite sharply defined. When they write of man, they are primarily thinking of two things. First, they are intent on reaching some conclusion concerning human frailty. There is a very close connection between the coercive functions of government and the human disposition to vice. An estimation of the strength of that disposition will naturally affect a theorist's views on the structure and relations of government. Second, and more positively, they wish to explore the capacities for moral goodness and creative excellence inherent in human nature. Their opinions on this matter will also affect their theory of the structure and relations of government. In both cases, the great question of what ends or purposes government should serve dominates their discussion. The allowance that must be made consists in the recognition of the restricted and essentially moralistic quality of their discussions, even though the form and tone of these discussions suggest an absolute ambition to speak the whole truth about human nature in all the complexity of its manifestations.

The interest of political theorists in general sociology is also selective. Two main questions figure. The first is, What must the nonpolitical institutions of society be, if the desired political system is to exist in a healthy condition over long periods of time? It is obvious that government does not stand alone, is not self-enclosed, but rather must be sustained by the practices and attitudes and even manners of the governed population. The way or style of life of a people is never neutral in its interaction with the political system. It can either subvert or nourish that system. The second question is, What institutions cooperate best with the political system to achieve the ends at which the system aims? If up to a certain point the values inherent in and issuing from the processes of a political system—values like justice, fairness, rationality, self-determination, continuity, the release of energy—appear to be sufficient and to exhaust the moral concerns of the political theorist advocating that system, other values soon appear that require the proper workings of nongovernmental institutions and practices if they too are to be realized. If certain kinds of human relations, certain kinds of human character, are to emerge, society as a whole must provide the suitable environment. As a result, the works of political theory are full of discussion of the family, sexuality, religion, the economy, art and literature, mores, and many things besides.

Among political theorists, the names of Plato, Aristotle, Montesquieu, and Rousseau may be mentioned as those for whom sociological questions are of the highest importance. The presence of this sociological interest is a sure indication of an overriding commitment to exploring the possibilities of human development, a refusal to remain satisfied with merely setting down the foundations for a morally acceptable political system. It would be wrong to minimize the achievement of those political theorists like Cicero, Aquinas, Locke, and Paine who seem to deal with sociological questions only incidentally, sometimes assuming that if government is healthy everything else will take care of itself, sometimes occupied so intensely with politics that all other matters fade from sight, sometimes looking upon society as fixed, and only government as capable of change. Their achievements require no apology; what they say about politics affords a basis for others who are more sociologically oriented to build upon. Nevertheless, it is obvious that political theories exhibit widely different amounts of richness: the richer ones are usually the more sociological ones.

To summarize, we can say that those works making up the body of political theory are all characterized by four traits: they are moral, inclusive, philosophical, and general. Only some are systematic. These works also vary in the range of their psychological and sociological speculation. In the species of moral writing about politics, we may distinguish between political theory and the following: ideology (which may be either simplified or debased political theory), the writings of political moralists (which, though moral, may not be inclusive, philosophical, or general, or may be one or two of those things but not all three), and the writings of moral philosophers and philosophical anthropologists (which though not directly political may be filled with import for politics and political thought of all kinds). Courses in the history of political theory are made up mostly of works in political theory, with a few ideologies (like Fascism and Stalinism), writings of political moralists (like Plutarch and Orwell), and implicitly political works of moral philosophy (like those by the late Stoics and the recent existentialists) added to the list. We now must examine the content of political theory in greater detail.

Chapter II

THE DISCUSSION OF ENDS
IN POLITICAL THEORY

We have already said that the fundamental moral question of politics
is, What ends or purposes should government serve? The literature of
political theory is made up of the answers to that question. Down through
time, numbers of men have taken upon themselves the burden of thought
about first and last things in politics. But they have not spoken with one
voice; indeed, political theory is famous for its contrasts. So emphatic do
these contrasts seem that the study of political theory can easily become
a game in which thinkers are placed in ready opposition to each other,
and each body of thought reduced to a slogan or a phrase. Justice or the
rule by philosophers is associated with Plato, the rule of law or the life
of virtue with Aristotle, peace with St. Augustine, power or political greatness with Machiavelli, constitutionalism or the protection of property with
Locke, direct democracy with Rousseau, the classless society with Marx,
and so on. There can be no doubt that this simple approach to the study
of political theory does reflect, though in a distorted way, the diversity
of responses that have been given to the same question. Political theorists
have been in conflict with each other, sometimes quite deliberately so.
Even where there has been agreement on the definition of the ends of

political life, there has been disagreement on the presuppositions and consequences of that definition. Political theories do not add up to one political theory; there seems to be no cumulative progress in the work of political theorists; the job of political theory never seems to get done; no theory secures the assent of thoughtful men, generation after generation.

Five Responses to Disagreement in Political Theory

What, then, is one to make of interminable disagreement? Several approaches suggest themselves.

The first approach is primarily an *esthetic* one. Confronted by a series of divergent political theories, one could celebrate that very divergence and find in it a source of inexhaustible interest. What matters is not the validity of the conclusions that theorists offer for acceptance, but the skill with which the conclusions are arrived at, the subtely of argumentation, the internal coherence of the theoretical work, the power or beauty either of specific parts of the work or of the work as a whole. One does not search for truth or moral guidance, or for relief from confusion, but for striking intellectual performances. One may assume that there is no such thing as moral truth, and that therefore validity of conclusions cannot be an appropriate standard by which to judge any political theory. Or one may assume that if there can be truth in moral matters, it will not be found, to any important degree, in works of political theory, but rather in common sense, worldly wisdom, or political science that does not pretend to be normative. One may look upon political theory as a species of metaphysics, metaphysics understood as the effort of the solitary thinker to discipline reality by forcing it into a pattern that answers to the metaphysician's own esthetic impulse, or to his intellectual will to power.

According to this approach, political theory, like anything beautiful, is essentially on the margin of life, a luxury to be enjoyed after the practicalities have been attended to, a form of play to be accepted playfully. This approach may be carried to the point of likening political theories to literary utopias, admired for their daring, but relegated to the category of fantasy. Or political theory may be seen as comparable to works of literary art, like novels and poems, capable of giving pleasure, but ruined when pressed into utilitarian service.

The second approach could be called *relativist*. The assumption here is that there is no absolute moral truth; perhaps the entire notion of moral truth is mistaken. Political theory is the emanation of historical conditions: if social reality does not automatically produce a basic political theory in consonance with the urgent needs of the whole society, or the needs of either the dominant or the "rising" class or group, it nevertheless circumscribes the range of possible political theory. And as conditions change, so must political theory. What appears to be moral disagreement is actually the successive discarding of obsolete moral ideas. The relevance of any political theory is confined to the time and place in which it comes to light. Its "truth" is only its adequacy in justifying the defense of, or the attack on, the established order. Consequently, the major use of studying political theory is to gain insight into the nature of a society or a historical period. The element of free creation in works of political theory is shown in minor ways, as in recommendations regarding dress or diet, as they may occur. For the rest, the political theorist, like the propagandist or the politician, but with more dignity, either consciously yields to overriding forces, or unwittingly accepts the presuppositions of political life that his contemporaries share. When there is a wide discrepancy between the theorist and his times, he is likely to be "romantic" in the bad sense— an archaist or futurist dreamer who, in his futility, is as much a prisoner of his historical situation as more realistic men—or some sort of satirist devoid of any pragmatic intention, except that of prodding his society into a heightened self-awareness.

Those who adopt the relativist approach may concede the extreme difficulty of using terms like "class" or "group" or "historical period" with precision: thinkers alive at the same time but living in different countries, or thinkers of the same nationality but separated by one generation or a few, may take part in the same discourse, may be determined in the same manner by their experience of social reality. But in any case, social reality is prior to thought; existent needs generate political theory. And we, alive in the present, better equipped than those before us to understand the decisive role of circumstance in molding consciousness, are not any the less subject to circumstance when we construct or appreciate or accept a political theory.

The third approach could be called the *plausibility* approach. According to this approach, almost all political theories can succeed, at least partially, in convincing the reader initially of their rightness, but they turn out to be unacceptable after closer investigation of the underlying moral *or* factual premises, or both. In case after case these premises are faulty. Only when these premises are granted—and they rarely can be —will these political theories stand up. Their plausibility stems from the common mastery of presentation found in the great works of political theory: an ability to carry the reader along, to hide or disguise their premises, to develop a train of thought fully and compellingly. But once a theorist has been plumbed to his depths, his work will, in all likelihood, be rejected. For example, if you grant to Plato that political rule requires metaphysical knowledge, that such knowledge is essentially incommunicable, that only a few men (those with gold in their souls) are capable of attaining it, and that they can attain it only after a rigorous training of the body, the senses, the desires, and the mind, then perhaps you would also grant him the necessity of absolute rule by philosophers. If you grant to Aristotle that only Greeks are capable of leading the life of virtue and hence are worthy of freedom, that the life of virtue is the life of happiness, and that for virtue to be permitted its indispensable political component, citizenship must be confined to those capable of leading the life of virtue, then perhaps you would also grant him his view that the ideal state would consist of a body of free citizens of Greek ancestry, living in conditions of leisure and material sufficiency made possible by the labor of the non-Greek slave or serf population. If you grant to Hobbes that the preservation of life is the highest political end, that life is threatened by the weakening of political order, and that the fierce competitiveness of men continuously weakens political order, then perhaps you would also grant him the necessity of the absolute and authoritarian sovereign state. If you grant to Locke that the preservation of human rights is the sole purpose of government, that most men (if protected) will go about their business in tranquility, and that the only source of domestic mischief is the absolute and authoritarian sovereign state, then perhaps you would also grant him the desirability of limited, constitutional rule.

But suppose that the assertions about human nature made by these theorists, their factual claims, are untenable. What is there to do but say that the moral disagreement among these theorists, and between each of these theorists and the impartial reader, is caused (in part anyway) by error? Scientific psychology and anthropology are not far advanced, but are they not far enough advanced to enable one to discredit the conceptions of human nature found in each of these political theories? Suppose also that one disputes Aristotle's insistence on political participation as a necessary ingredient of the virtuous life, or Hobbes's elevation of life itself above all other values, or Locke's concentration on the individual as the center of the moral universe. One could say that these men hold wrong moral beliefs: in the light of one's own beliefs theirs are to be condemned. Or one could say that all beliefs are arbitrary, and that every man can believe what he wants. But he should not think he can rationally persuade someone else of the rightness of his position. Moral beliefs have no connection to rational persuasion or to proof; there is no way of judging the merits of competing beliefs; beliefs are an expression of the feelings of the person holding those beliefs, and nothing more. All statements of moral belief, at whatever length or of whatever ingenuity, remain subjective and are equally entitled to a hearing or to no hearing at all. When there is moral disagreement, no resolution is possible; there can be only silence or warfare.

Or one could say that it is in the very nature of moral matters that men disagree with each other, that these matters are "essentially contested." Life is so complex, the individual can comprehend such a small part of it, each man's experience is such a tiny fragment of all possible experience, temperaments vary so much, moral judgment is so tricky and inconclusive, that it is no wonder the history of moral thought, and thus of political theory, is riddled with contention. The proper attitude is one of gratitude to the series of political theorists who have taken the trouble to work out their positions. They have enriched the world by showing where numerous fundamental moral beliefs can lead; they have carried moral articulateness very far. After we have chosen, inscrutably as it were, our general outlook on political life, we then can consult a political theory for the careful completion of that outlook. That is the great benefit of studying political theories. And that is the only benefit one can legitimately expect, given the unalterably problematic quality of moral judgment.

The fourth approach is *dogmatic*. Starting with a firm assurance that one's own system of moral beliefs is the only correct system, one may then brand all other systems as erroneous. It need not be thought that the whole truth is to be found in the writings of a single political theorist. Rather, one may say that a certain tradition, which has perhaps evolved through time while staying faithful to a few basic principles or a few articles of religious faith, contains the truth. Other traditions show error in its multiplicity. Moral certitude may derive from the acceptance of religious writings as genuinely divine revelation, or from certitude about "the nature of things" as disclosed by metaphysics or natural science or some combination of both. Those who take the dogmatic approach may concede that even with divine help, or the help of philosophical or scientific genius, human intelligence cannot attain perfect insight into God's will or the nature of things: the act of faith or a measure of skeptical reserve is acknowledgment of human limitation in the face of God's ultimate unknowability or the final impenetrability of nature. Furthermore, many difficulties beset the effort to translate religious or metaphysical or scientific knowledge—which is often highly abstract or general, and sometimes obscure—into moral precepts suitable to guide political life. But the effort must be made; it is really the only effort worthy of the moral man when he sets his mind to political matters. Within the confines of the same system, men will disagree on specific applications to political life—on the correct assessment of a ruler, a practice, a policy, or an act. Equally well-intentioned men, pledged to the same faith or view, may not be equally enlightened or experienced. There must be an authority whose competence to resolve disagreement is accepted by the disputants. Also, as historical conditions change, new interpretations of abstract knowledge are pressed, and may indeed be necessary. Through all changes, however, fidelity to revelation or metaphysics or science can be kept.

As for erroneous political theories, the important question is not, Can anything be learned even from those in error? but, What leads men into error? Many dogmatists claim that at least the rudiments of correct moral judgment are natural to man; but several things can blight the original endowment, such as self-interest, intellectual pride, the misfortune of living in a society long since lapsed into, but now habituated to, its error. In any case, the dependence of political theory on some larger understanding of the world is stressed; and correct political theory can be derived only from correct assumptions about the world. The fight about political theory is part of the greater struggle about the meaning of human existence, though it may well be that part which is most interestingly symptomatic and most directly relevant to ordinary life. Some dogmatists say that erroneous political theories can be actually poisonous if they gain sufficient adherence. The study of political theory should not be seen as a polite affair: ideas have consequences.

The fifth approach is *eclectic,* and turns on the notion that every tradition of political theory—probably every political theorist—is partly right and partly wrong. Political wisdom consists in acquainting oneself with the whole range of political thought, dismissing none of it. If, on the other hand, one at last consents to a particular political theory, the consent must be given in a spirit of humility. One must say that *on balance* the approved political theory is stronger than its competitors. All political theories are to be judged by one standard, by their closeness to the goal of formulating the principles and envisaging the practices needed to realize a way of life, or nurture a kind of human character, to which one is committed. Political theories characteristically emphasize some things while slighting or ignoring others. It may be that no political theory can ever avoid these disproportions: no theorist, no matter how great, can be free of bias or misplaced enthusiasms or blindness to some aspects of life. When one chooses a theory, or a tradition of theory, one must therefore be aware of its shortcomings. Furthermore, a price must be paid for everything; even one's ideal will entail the sacrifice or abridgment of some values, because they are incompatible or uneasy with it. For example, one may cherish human equality and still retain admiration for the aristocratic ethos. A society must choose between them; it cannot have both at the same time. The virtue of adversary political theories is to keep us aware of the losses we sustain as we implement an ideal, or merely subscribe to an ideal in the abstract. No odium, except in rare cases, will attach to those who are in moral disagreement with oneself over the questions of political theory. The truth has been hard to get at; and though we think we now have it, we will not scorn those who have failed. They too contribute to moral understanding.

Some eclectics would endeavor to piece the truth together from heterogeneous theories. They refuse to believe that a political theory has to be accepted or rejected in its entirety, or that its truth is inextricably joined to its error, or that its component elements are so related as to make each of them meaningful only in the presence of the rest and incapable of importation into some other structure of moral thought about politics. One tradition of political theory may be preponderantly truthful from the moral point of view, or possess more of the truth than any other tradition. But the judicious student will learn from all or nearly all traditions. As time goes on, clarity is reached on an ever larger area of moral matters; some views are put aside as fallacious. Widespread agreement is not reached, but some gross confusions are destroyed. The gratitude to all political theorists is not limitless; admiration for their hard work does not mean indifference to their mistakes. Nevertheless, if one is, say, a liberal, one will not simply respect the sincerity of the conservative and tolerate his advocacy of it; one will also absorb some conservatism for the sake of enriching liberalism. In conservatism will be found reminders of *truths* (perhaps unpleasant) that no one can afford to overlook; there will be restraints on one's excesses. The same eclecticism is suitable for the conservative and others as well. Moral disagreement is a sign of human vitality responding to social complexity.

A Rejoinder to All Five Responses

These then are five possible approaches to the record of moral disagreement that comprises the history of political theory. We have tried to state them with as much fairness as possible. What is important is not to search for examples of these approaches, but to compress points of view that appear explicitly or implicitly in the writings of political theorists themselves, and in works of commentary and criticism. At this point, our purpose is not to decide between the approaches. To borrow from the eclectics, all the approaches contain some truths, contain some of the truth. They also share some arguments. For all their cogency, however, one significant truth eludes them. All political theorists, consciously or not, agree that if a political theory is to be worthy of general consideration, if it is to conform to the standards of moral argument, if it is to be something other than an expression of whimsy or eccentricity, the theorist must sincerely strive to defend principles of government which, if made actual in the real world, would achieve *the common good*. The phrase may not be part of the vocabulary of a political theorist, but when it is not, it will readily be seen that the concept is implicit. Every political theorist commonly studied in courses in political theory believes that all his advocacy is ultimately in the name of the common good. This consideration sets limits on the scope of moral disagreement between political theorists. Much disagreement there certainly is, disagreement of the most profound sort. But the disagreement takes place within an accepted framework, and is all the more interesting for that reason. The record of political theory assumes an altered aspect when we see that behind its wonderful diversity there is allegiance to a single aim: to envisage a political system that works to the common good.

When, therefore, we come across a political theorist who quite clearly rejects the standard of the common good, we must be careful to notice that he is not making a moral argument which accords with the conventions of moral argument. His disagreement with other political theorists is totally different from the disagreement which the other political theorists have among themselves. Nietzsche, a writer whose system of thought contained much of political relevance, defied the common good, and championed instead the good of a tiny elite at the expense of the great mass of men. (This is a crude way of putting it, but Nietzsche is frequently taken to stand for this position.) He is not to be denied inclusion in the company of political theorists or political moralists because he substituted a peculiar heroism for the common good. He must, however, be seen as an exception. He must be seen as he saw himself, as one who was an immoralist, transvaluing all values, embarking on a journey beyond good and evil. He placed himself beyond the pale of moral argument; he did not write to gain *general* assent. He set himself against *all* the inherited traditions of moral thought.

The problem then becomes to explain why political theory is full of disagreement when political theorists agree that the common good is the end or purpose that government should serve. The fact that they disagree on almost everything while agreeing on the ultimate standard will lose its oddness when we recall analogous situations in other human activities. All legal systems are dedicated to justice, yet vary enormously in their procedures. All societies inculcate virtue, yet produce remarkably dissimilar forms of behavior. All metaphysicians seek truth, yet propound conflicting doctrines. Other examples could be given. The temptation is to conclude, however, that the ultimate standard, in each case, is a concept empty of meaning, but so hallowed in the minds of men, so full of favorable connotations, that everyone gives it token adherence and then goes on to say or do absolutely anything he wants. What supposedly matters, in each case, is not the vacuous ultimate standard but the specific arguments (in metaphysical systems) and the specific practices (in legal systems and social codes of virtue). Similarly, that almost all political theorists protest their devotion to the common good is a fact of no importance. They are to be judged, if judged at all, by the detailed recommendations they make concerning forms of government, the powers and scope of governmental authority, the rights and duties of citizens, and other such political features.

The inclination to dispose of the concept of the common good in this fashion must be resisted. Of course, the concept lends itself to manipulation, to insincere uses. Of course, the concept can be made to entail many kinds of political arrangements or practices, even when sincerity is present. This is only to acknowledge that the concept of the common good is on the highest level of abstraction. It is in the nature of such concepts that men will, with the best intentions in the world, interpret them differently and by doing so will arrive at heterogeneous conclusions. The important point is that the concept of the common good will, despite its abstraction, exclude some lesser political principles, some political arrangements and practices. The concept is wide, but not infinitely permissive. At least, it will exclude arbitrary rule, the punishment of the innocent, unfair distribution of sacrifices, enslavement of people admittedly equal in moral capacity with the enslavers, continuously ignorant political leadership, corrigible poverty. It will exclude the unprincipled neglect, exploitation, or sacrifice of some for the benefit of others. It will exclude maxims like "Might makes right" and "Some men can be treated as means only." Again, these exclusions may appear to be so vaguely worded as to permit almost anything if a clever enough argument is put forth in its behalf. But after a while the cleverness will be seen through. There are limits to verbal ingenuity. To think otherwise is to abandon the very possibility of rationality, not only in moral matters, but in all sorts of discourse.

If the common good excludes a number of practices, we must not expect to find them elaborated and defended in the literature of political theory (except by an occasional immoralist). If the common good excludes a number of lesser or "lower-order" principles, we must not expect to find them articulated and urged for acceptance. We can expect to find, and do find, competing interpretations of the concept of the common good and consequently widely divergent sets of political recommendations. Besides, even when two or more theorists understand the common good in the same way, their political proposals may be quite discrepant, so problematic is political life, so tenuous is the connection between an ultimate standard and its concrete applications.

Definitions of the Common Good

What then is the common good—what is the good common to all men which the government of a society exists to promote? There have been several main answers to this question, at least as many as to the question, What is the good life for the individual? It cannot be said that each culture or epoch has produced only one answer. At the same time and place, political theorists have conceived of the common good quite disparately. The content of the concept is not *historically* determined. If one insists on knowing why rough contemporaries like Bentham and Burke wrote on the common good as they did and wrote contrastingly, one must look to their biographies. But how pale and small are personal considerations in comparison to their writings considered as public statements—indeed, as public acts. We must take the existence of various interpretations of the common good as a fact of the greatest interest, the psychological explanation of which is only of some slight interest. On the other hand, as we shall see, there is much that *is* historically determined in all political theories, much that seems the product of the time, an extension of its tendencies, or a disclosure of its promise. The way in which a political theorist defines the common good is not, however, subject to a historically determinist analysis.

It is usually possible to express in a word or a phrase what is considered the common good in the work of every political theorist. The word or phrase would be the name of some political value which, if established in society, would be to the advantage of all members of that society. The value would, in fact, be the greatest of all possible political values; it would be the *highest* value able to be shared by all, and to be shared by all as the result of the proper operation of the political system as conceived by the theorist. None of the purportedly supreme values that appear in the works of political theory is startling or incidental to the life of man. The originality of a political theorist is not shown by reference to his conception of the common good, but rather to its elaboration and defense, and to what he makes follow from that conception. We could say, for example, that Plato thought that order defined the common good; Aristotle (in the ideal state), the life of virtuous citizenship; Cicero, justice; St. Augustine, peace; St. Thomas, order; Machiavelli, the preservation and greatness of one's country; Hobbes, peace; Locke, the preservation of the person (in the extended sense to include possessions); Rousseau, the life of virtuous citizenship; Hegel, the preservation and greatness of one's country; Bentham, the greatest possible pleasure of each; Burke, order; Madison, justice; Mill, freedom; Dewey, the facilitation of social change; and so on.

Doubtless these ascriptions could be questioned. Political theorists are not themselves always clear about the hierarchy of their values. It is not, however, of crucial importance to insist that this rather than that is the value which the theorist cherishes above every other. We read a political theorist for his whole argument. But for rough purposes, to identify each theorist with a supreme value defining the common good, as we have done, is not seriously misleading. The main point is that, clearly or not, each theorist is out to achieve a net political result which in his opinion is to everybody's advantage or benefit; and is, at the same time, the most desirable that can be attained, and worth any cost that must be paid by omitting or compromising other values.

We must stress that the common good is a *political* value; it is the purpose or end which *government* should serve. The essential sphere of governmental activity is the network of those relations between people which are amenable to political regulation. All the values posited as the common good are values pertaining to the quality of these relations, though they may turn out to be instrumental to values more important than themselves. The common good need not be the highest good in life, but it is the highest good in political life.

arrangement is foolproof, but normally such restraints or devices can be relied on.

The great division in this category of theorists is between those who confine rule to one man or a few, and those who accord to the people a share of power. It is a fact that every political theory for the past one hundred and fifty years has been preoccupied with the question of popular participation—whether to resist it, admit it slowly and grudgingly, or welcome it enthusiastically. The growth of the popular idea has directly resulted from the growth of wealth and from the advances in the techniques of social interchange which reflect the growth of wealth and stimulate it. The point made by some is that as ever larger numbers of men acquire material sufficiency, they acquire concurrently that modicum of rationality which entitles them to full, or a fuller, citizenship. With sufficiency comes self-control—not altruism, but common-sense awareness of self-interest and the relation of self-interest to the interest of others. At the same time, society can afford investment in education and other welfarist measures, all of which civilize human nature, or at least tame it adequately for the purposes of popular politics. The liberals, the democrats, and some constitutionalists say or imply such things.

Those who resist popular politics do so for many reasons, but two stand out. First, they do not yet see the promise implicit in the growth of wealth; specifically, industrialism has not yet developed. Second, even though industrialism has developed, it can never alter the basic incapacity or irrationality of men in the mass. The highest political end, the common good, cannot therefore be defined as freedom, or the facilitation of social change; it must be defined as the preservation of order. The kind of order to be preserved is that of a class-stratified society, in which political power must remain in the hands of a few whose wealth promotes a style of life indispensable to the proper use of power, or of a few who alone have the talents—which only a few can have—indispensable to the proper use of power. But though power may be denied to the many, the many nevertheless sustain the order through their good will and docility, not merely through fear and superstition. Aquinas, Calvin, and, in modern times, Burke and his heirs champion order as the common good on the basis of arguments like these.

When it comes to the worth of worldly things, all these theorists—Christian, deist, agnostic—show similarities. They all accord reality to the normal aspirations of men, no matter how fervid their belief in a supernatural realm, or how tinged their thoughts are by reflection on the caprice of human affairs and the shortness of human life. To assert the primacy of freedom, justice, the preservation of rights, or the facilitation of social change is to assert that the protection of worldly things is a task honorable enough for the fierce exertions required to keep a political system functioning as it is supposed to. The emphasis changes from theorist to theorist, but the value of property, civil liberty, orderly and regular justice is clearly endorsed. That is to say, the components of a secure, perhaps happy, life are placed at the heart of political reckoning. The proof of this sentiment is found in the fact that all these theorists allow for the use of violence to achieve either a restoration of a political system that has been damaged by the encroachments of arrogant rulers, or the initiation of a political system that promises to make good the demands that men may legitimately make of a political system but which are not met by the existing one. To be sure, there is no wanton preaching of violence, no enthusiastic theory of violence. Some theorists, like the Thomists and the Calvinists, hedge the right of revolution with severe restrictions and implicitly give the benefit of the doubt to established authority. But they also make clear that there are limits to what the people should endure. Though disruption and violence are to be lamented, and necessarily involve men in wrongdoing, certain values justify men in extreme measures. These values pertain not only to the expression of conscience and the worship of God, but also to the worldly life of men. Other theorists, like Locke, Burke, and Paine, are less severe in their restrictions, and discuss the problem of revolutionary violence wholly apart from the sacred needs of religious life.

The theorists we have placed in the second category have widely divergent views on the value of public things as opposed to private things. They all conceive of the political system as the source of many blessings, but join to their conception several attitudes that set them at odds with each other. Their attitudes toward three different matters are relevant: first, the moral quality of the institution of government; second, the moral quality of political participation; and third, the relation between the ends directly served by the proper workings of government and the ends made possible.

There are two paramount positions on the moral quality of the institution of government. One holds that there is no need at all to apologize for the necessity of having government. Government, as described by Cicero, the Thomists, the Calvinists, the *philosophes*, Burke, Madison, Green, Dewey, and others, is a totally sensible contrivance for human wants and purposes. Human life is unimaginable without it, though lip service may be given to the loveliness of an anarchic condition at the beginning or end of time. The mere operation of government, when it is as it is supposed to be, embodies a number of moral values, such as rationality, justice, fairness; indeed, Cicero and Thomas see it as the earthly approximation of godlike behavior. These moral values are not even to be found except in the operation of government; they have no other locus. Such a position comports well with the sorts of moderate expectations these theorists have for government.

The other position is found in the constitutionalist tradition of Locke, the libertarian tradition of Paine and Jefferson, and the liberal tradition of Spencer. It is most passionately expressed by Paine, who said in *Common Sense* that "government, even in its best state, is but a necessary evil. . . . Government, like dress, is the badge of lost innocence; the palaces of kings are built upon the ruins of the bowers of paradise."[1] The sentiment is echoed in the common phrase that that government is best which governs least. The explanation for the existence of government is found not in general human necessity and aspiration but in the tendency of some men, if not all, to transgress against their fellows. Vice is the source of government, and thus government is a *shameful* necessity. The public realm is inherently despicable: men's dependence on it should not restrain them from viewing it with radical suspiciousness. When it works well, the people should be barely aware of it: its importance is negative. Social relations—that is, the sum of nonpolitical relations—carry forward the real work of mankind. By reasoning in this way, these theorists manage to combine aversion to government with expectations of it that are more than minimal.

Closely related are the conclusions on the moral quality of political participation. What should one think of the role of the man of public affairs, and also of the role of citizen? On the role of the man of affairs, the statesman, Cicero, Aquinas, Calvin, the *philosophes*, Burke, and Madison speak with great deference, sometimes with awe. They underline the burdensome and morally treacherous life which the statesman—if he is a moral man—must lead. When he performs his role in accordance with the highest standards, he performs a role that is second to none in moral dignity. At least, it is second to none except for that of priest or minister. It is a role worthy of the best men. And when the best men fill it, order or justice, the common good, will be forthcoming. On the other hand, the difficulties of statesmen do not preoccupy Locke and Paine and Spencer and the traditions stemming from them. Because it is primarily negative, the task of government should not weigh heavily. It is open to ordinary talents. By thus minimizing government, these writers can depreciate public things and still define the common good as something more than mere peace.

Furthermore, some liberal and all democratic writers make much of the office of citizenship, advocating as they do the institution of representative government. This necessarily sets limits to the extent to which they can in fact depreciate public things, at the same time that it sets limits to the extent to which they feel compelled to depreciate public things. Citizen participation provides a safeguard for the good behavior of those in power, and thereby makes power less fearful. The office of citizenship is a political necessity. More than that, Paine and Jefferson

---

[1] Thomas Paine, *Common Sense*, in Harry Hayden Clark (ed.), *Thomas Paine, Representative Selections* (New York: Hill and Wang, 1961), p. 4.

invest it with genuine moral value. Paine, for instance, speaks of "the gigantic manliness" fostered by a political system resting on the involvement, though indirect, of the people. On the other hand, among the nonliberal and nondemocratic theorists in this category, the concept of citizenship is hardly in evidence (except in the thought of Cicero and Madison, who mix popular and elitist tendencies). Their lofty evaluation of the moral quality of political participation is based almost exclusively on the labor of rulers when they are guided by the correct principles, when they are enlightened.

The relation between the ends directly served by the proper workings of government and the ends made possible is a vast subject, including in itself a large portion of moral speculation about politics. We can touch on it only briefly. All the theorists in the second category, even those who place considerable value on public things, commit themselves to a belief in the inestimable worth of private activity. The division among them can be represented in the following way.

Some theorists say or imply that the fundamental unit of private life is the group, be it the family or the occupation. The values of private life are those of domesticity or craftsmanship, or both. For most people, the richness of reality—insofar as life on earth can be rich—comes from immersion in the everyday. The highest purpose of government, the common good, is to secure the framework within which everyday life can proceed as unprecariously as possible. Politics is only a means; the end is nonpolitical; it is private, or social. (The Thomists and the Calvinists say that beyond securing everyday life, there is one purpose higher still— the promotion of the true faith—and that promotion takes place in subordinate assistance to spiritual authority.) The genuine task of government is not ceaseless activity in behalf of private life, but a benign superintendence and protection of activities that go on more or less free from outside direction. Some amount of paternalism is advocated, but it is marginal.

Some theorists, and Locke is the first major one, see the individual as the fundamental unit of private life. The interests of the individual are the touchstone of governmental activity, and are the supreme values of life. Interests are clothed in the language of rights, the natural right of every man to life, liberty, and property. Government is the servant of the aggregation of men. It performs that service mainly through forbearance, through abstention from meddling with the individual as he pursues his ends. Once government secures his rights, it has done all it is competent to do, and all it has any warrant to do. Or, as Bentham would say, once government clears the way for the pursuit of legitimate self-interest, it has done its job.

Some theorists, beginning in the late eighteenth and the nineteenth centuries, and Mill is the most important, also see the individual as the fundamental unit of private life. But the theory of indefeasible natural rights gives way to a concern for the cultivation of personality, or "individuality" as Mill calls it. Government continues to be primarily abstentionist and is judged by its tolerance, by its commitment to freedom. Only in a condition of maximum freedom can individuality flourish. The highest end in life is the free individual who is permitted to become "a noble and beautiful object of contemplation."[2] To make freedom meaningful, education is the absolute prerequisite. To serve the cause of freedom best, government should "require and compel the education, up to a certain standard, of every human being who is born its citizen."[3] It should not insist on public education for all, but it should insist that all be educated. That is its great duty; and by discharging that duty, it acknowledges the primacy of private ends, and most adequately exemplifies the instrumental nature of politics.

Some theorists, beginning with the welfare-liberals in the latter part of the nineteenth century, subscribe to the view that the individual's benefit is the highest of all moral values and understand benefit to be all that conduces to self-realization, much as Mill does. However, two changes differentiate them from Mill. First, they expand the role of government to take in the continuous implementation of policies that relieve suffering and lessen poverty, that "remove the obstacles" (in T. H. Green's phrase) to full self-realization. Government ceases to be abstentionist; freedom itself will be interfered with, if necessary, to make freedom more meaningful. For countenancing large-scale interference, Dewey can be said to have replaced freedom as the content of the common good with some other value. We have chosen to call that value "the facilitation of social change" in order to indicate his wish that government be restlessly sensitive to the needs of self-realization. Social life is in constant flux, and government must be prepared both to rescue the individual from the onrush of events and to guide those events in the right direction, to the utmost of its ability. Second, Green and Dewey give up the traditional liberal image of the individual as isolated and wholly self-reliant. They cherish the individual above everything, but emphasize the interdependence of individuals. Individuals do not exist in isolation, morally or any other way. They are what they are because of the society in which they were born and raised. They do not make themselves. Their pursuits are pursuits undertaken with others. Green says, "When we speak of freedom as something to be so highly prized, we mean a positive power or capacity of doing or enjoying something

---

[2] John Stuart Mill, *On Liberty*, in *Utilitarianism, Liberty and Representative Government* (New York: E. P. Dutton, 1950), p. 161.

[3] *Ibid.*, p. 216.

worth doing or enjoying, and that, too, something that we do or enjoy in common with others."[4] This general sense of man as a social creature makes it easier for Green, Dewey, and their successors to conceive of government as an active agency, rather than as simply a preserver, a deterrent of wrongdoing. There is no worship of government; it furthers ends greater than any it embodies or achieves. But it does further them: it does not only indirectly permit them to emerge. We may say that Green and Dewey, aided by some in the Kantian, Hegelian, and Marxist traditions, develop the idea of individuality, the idea of *person*, which is only sketched, though brilliantly, by Mill. They try to answer such questions as, What must social conditions be if men as they pass from childhood are to become persons? What must social conditions be if the needs of men as persons are to be satisfied? What sorts of treatment at the hands of government are persons entitled to, from the point of view of political and legal procedure? What is to be morally expected of a person in the form of duties and obligations? By raising such issues, they find ways of honoring Mill's commitment while altering his notion of government's contribution to it.

In sum, there are many roads that lead to the second category in which we have placed political theorists, just as there are many conceptions of the common good present in this category. What allies these theorists is their common sense. In any case there can be no doubt that the political life of the Western world derives most of its intellectual content from the continuous interplay of the ideas of the theorists in this category.

The main writers in the third category are Plato, Aristotle, Machiavelli, Rousseau, and Hegel. They (and their followers) bring to man's political life the greatest expectations; they make it support a staggering moral weight. When political life is ideally what it should be, men are thereby put in touch with a reality higher in seriousness or meaning than any other, with the exception (made by Plato, Aristotle, and some in the Hegelian tradition) of a contemplative reality. The relations of ideal politics, the structures and processes of ideal politics, embody values superior to any private ones they may permit or promote. The common good, the ultimate political value, is the preservation of the political system. Its preservation is the preservation of crucial moral opportunities. If politics can be said to be instrumental, it is instrumental to the perfection of character. It is directly instrumental: without involvement in its activities, character cannot become perfect. Participation in political life calls forth the fullest virtue. To be sure, the political system is expected to attend to the usual concerns of ordinary life. But politics is not ex-

---

[4] T. H. Green, "Liberal Legislation and Freedom of Contract," in John R. Rodman (ed.), *The Political Theory of T. H. Green* (New York: Appleton-Century-Crofts, 1964), pp. 51–52.

hausted by the services it performs. Its full measure is taken when we see it above all as the medium for transcendent human excellence of one kind or another.

The key to this position is obviously the view taken of the value of public things as opposed to all private things. There is no human endeavor in the world to compare with participation in the ideal political system. (When the political system is not ideal, the virtuous man seeks his fulfillment outside the political system and does so either because he wants to avoid contamination from imperfect politics or because he will generally be denied the chance to take part.) Plato, Aristotle, Machiavelli, Rousseau, and Hegel are all in agreement on this valuation. On the *reasons* for prizing public things, as well as on other matters, they show enormous differences from each other.

Why then does each thinker hold the broadest possible conception of the common good? Why does each thinker expect the maximum from the working of the ideal political system? In the case of Plato and Hegel, the premise is that the ideal political system is, in effect, the realization of some supreme universal principle. For Plato, the system described in *The Republic* would be, if established in some polis, the outward manifestation of the abstract idea of justice. The reign of justice would still the intolerable flux of political life. Right relations between men would be achieved, and the cruelty, selfishness, and blindness common to the varieties of imperfect politics abolished. Society would be, at least approximately, in accord with metaphysical reason, with the underlying rationality of the world. "In heaven," says Socrates, "there is laid up a pattern of it [the ideal state] methinks, which he who desires may behold. . . ."[5] Correspondingly, Plato continuously disparages all the aims that unphilosophical men pursue, whether these aims are selfishly public or selfishly private, from honor to gain to appetitive satisfaction to naked domination. To be sure, these desires can never be totally abolished, even in the ideal state. But they can be tempered and regulated; and thus tempered and regulated, they do not interfere with the realization of a just order, but rather are made to contribute to it. Their abatement in the name of the just order, whatever the feelings of the great mass of unphilosophical people, is in no sense a sacrifice of anything worth preservation: men dine on a "mess of shadows."

For Hegel, "The state is the actuality of the ethical Idea. . . . The development of the state to constitutional monarchy is the achievement of the modern world, a world in which the substantial Idea has won the infinite form . . . the history of this genuine formation of ethical life is the content of the whole course of world-history. . . . The nation state is mind in its substantive rationality and immediate actuality and is there-

---

[5] Plato, *The Republic* (592), in *The Dialogues of Plato*, trans. Benjamin Jowett (2 vols., New York: Random House, n.d.), vol. I, p. 851.

fore the absolute power on earth."[6] In his *Philosophy of History*, Hegel projects a view of the pattern of human history, in which the entire human career is seen as the gradual, painful, and inevitable progression in the realization of the idea of human freedom, going from the Oriental stage to the Greek and then to the Roman, and culminating, at last, in the perfection of the Germanic (and Christian) stage. The institutional articulation of the last and highest stage is constitutional monarchy: a graded and stratified society, which has representative institutions, and at the apex of which is the institution of a wise, benevolent, and harmonizing monarchy. The purpose of history, from the start and through all its suffering and confusion, was to arrive at the society Hegel describes in *The Philosophy of Right*, a society that is, one might say, both the rationalized and the romanticized version of the Prussian monarchy of Hegel's day. To live with full awareness in such a society is to be implicated in the triumph of the rationality of the world. Correspondingly, Hegel argues that in comparison to the survival of the state in power and honor, the individual's interests are distinctly secondary. "Sacrifice on behalf of the individuality of the state is the substantial tie between the state and all its members and so is a universal duty."[7] The rigors and perils of the state's relations with other states disclose the essential "vanity of temporal good and concerns."[8] Duty transcends all private and group ("corporate") pursuits and concerns.

It must be acknowledged that Cicero and St. Thomas also look on the right political order as the human embodiment of supreme universal principle. The Ciceronian right political order accords with the mind of Nature; the Thomist with the will of God. But in neither of these theorists is the effort of connecting the proposed political system to a supreme universal principle so relentlessly carried out. Both writers are painfully aware of the tremendous obstacles an infirm human nature and a clouded human understanding place in the way of achieving any ideal. Their main moral endeavor consists in improving their inherited frameworks, and supplying for each framework an added consecration by reference to Nature or to God. There is very little *magic*, so to speak, in their political vision, very little pretentiousness. In their fascination with detailed recommendations, they often lose sight of their overarching intellectual construction. To live in the political systems they envisage is to share in something morally excellent, but it is not to share in an enterprise nearly as sublime as Plato's Republic or Hegel's constitutional monarchy.

As for the theorists of the divine right of monarchy, say, James I of England, or for Christian moralists like St. Paul who claim that "the

---

[6] G. W. F. Hegel, *Philosophy of Right*, trans. T. M. Knox (Oxford: Clarendon Press, 1942), pp. 155, 176, 212.
[7] *Ibid.*, p. 210.
[8] *Ibid.*

powers that be are ordained of God," some of the same considerations hold. To link rule with the will of God is, above everything else, a device to promote obedience. James I speaks of the monarch as receiving his power directly from God, and becoming thereby "God's Lieutenant" or "God's Minister." He is entitled to complete acceptance of his commands, except when his commands are unlawful. In that case, the most allowed to the subject is "eschewing and flying his [the king's] fury in his unlawful [commands], without resistance, but by sobbes and teares to God."[9] St. Paul speaks of the ruler in this way:

> For he is the minister of God to thee for good. But if thou do that which is evil, be afraid; for he beareth not the sword in vain: for he is the minister of God, a revenger to execute wrath upon him that doeth evil.[10]

But for these writers, as for the Augustinian and Lutheran traditions in political theory, obedience secures peace, and peace makes possible what really matters: the godly life, which is not public or political. St. Paul, St. Augustine, and Luther make it clear that the godly life can be lived in any society, provided there is peace, whereas for Plato and Hegel (contemplation aside), to participate, in whatever way, in the right political order is to have one's life transformed.

A different mode of praise for the political order is to be found in the writings of Aristotle, Machiavelli, and Rousseau. It could be said that Plato and Hegel see the excellence of their political systems as residing in a fixed pattern of human relations. All classes make their contribution to that excellence, either through governance or military service, or through mere obedience to rule and labor in the maintenance of the economic functions that sustain life. On the other hand, Aristotle, Machiavelli, and Rousseau make the chance for political involvement the differentiating characteristic of the ideal political system. For the three writers, active citizenship is intrinsic to the definition of the good man. The ideal political order is primarily the arena for virtue, for the highest kind of virtue. To preserve it is to preserve the network of activities that form the most morally significant segment of the good life. The stress is on *activity*—or to use a more modern-sounding word, *process*. It is not on pattern. Indirect participation through obedience, duty, and professional or vocational competence does not suffice. The common good is the preservation of the reality of virtue, the soul of which is public or political.

What then is the nature of virtue in each case? What is it that political involvement, far more than any other kind of involvement, elicits

---

9 James I of England, *The Trew Law of Free Monarchies,* in *Introduction to Contemporary Civilization in the West* (2 vols., 3rd ed., New York: Columbia University Press, 1960), vol. I, p. 928.

10 *Romans,* 13:4.

from human beings? What does it contribute to the formation of character? Aristotle, Machiavelli, and Rousseau are clear in their insistence that the political order they envisage is possible only in a city state. Positive citizenship can be open to all only if the number of citizens is small, and all three agree that all free men should be citizens. The point is reinforced by Aristotle's comment that the state must be small enough for the citizens to "know each other's characters"[11] and by Rousseau's statement that "It is necessary to confine and limit our interest and compassion in order to make it active."[12]

Aristotle's view is that the fullness of virtue requires the exercise of practical wisdom. In the *Nicomachean Ethics,* he defines practical wisdom as a "reasoned and true state of capacity to act with regard to human goods."[13] Without political involvement, practical wisdom could not have the occasion to display itself. It is a "mistake" to suppose that political involvement is just like the management of an estate or the running of a household: the former calls into play responsibilities of a larger scope and higher dignity than the other two.[14] Furthermore, merely voting in the general legislative assembly does not exhaust practical wisdom. ". . . The virtue of a good *ruler* [emphasis supplied] is the same as that of the good man. . . ."[15] To be a ruler or a statesman entails "political wisdom" in its entirety; "this has to do with action and deliberation, for a decree is a thing to be carried out in the form of an individual act." In the ideal political society, all citizens take turns in ruling, in performing those acts of deliberation and execution. And those acts naturally look to the well-being of the ideal political society, which is the preservation of all those conditions that permit citizens to lead a *contemplative* life, the best life for all men able to lead it. Thus, though the life of political activity is not itself the best life, it is both an indispensable ingredient of virtue and the practical guarantee of virtue's crown, the contemplative life.

In *The Social Contract,* Rousseau reasons in a manner similar to that of Aristotle, but adds some interesting elements of his own. The citizen in the ideal political society must take part, in his own person, in the legislative function. That function contains within it all that is needed for Rousseau's conception of virtue to be realized. Rousseau is adamant on the moral unacceptability of representative political institutions: they

---

[11] Aristotle, *Politics* (VII, 4), trans. Benjamin Jowett, in Richard McKeon (ed.), *The Basic Works of Aristotle* (New York: Random House, 1941), p. 1284.

[12] Jean Jacques Rousseau, "A Discourse on Political Economy," in Rousseau, *The Social Contract and Discourses,* trans. G. D. H. Cole (New York: E. P. Dutton, 1950), p. 301.

[13] Aristotle, *Nicomachean Ethics* (VI, 5), trans. W. D. Ross, in Richard McKeon, *op. cit.,* p. 1027.

[14] Aristotle, *Politics* (I, 1), in Richard McKeon, *op. cit.,* p. 1127.

[15] *Ibid.* (III, 4), p. 1181.

establish a remoteness from decision-making that mortally impairs virtue. To be represented is to alienate one's will; to alienate one's will is to become a slave. Man must take part in the process by which law is made; otherwise, he will live by a will that is not his own, he will not be free. In addition, taking part in the law-making process offers the supreme opportunity to practice benevolence, to do good toward one's fellows. To vote in accordance with the requirements of justice is the greatest conceivable act of benevolence. In sum, to help make the law by which one is bound, and to help make just laws, is to achieve the status of "moral liberty," a status that alone is adequate for a full humanity, and a status that is possible in the ideal city-state sketched in *The Social Contract*.

Machiavelli's theory also insists on the connection between citizenship and virtue. But Machiavelli's idea of virtue (virtù) is not that of Aristotle, Rousseau, or indeed of any conventional moralist. In his *Discourses of Livy*, the true quality of Machiavelli's ideals becomes clear. Their affinity to certain Greek and Roman ideals—that is, to pre-Christian ideals—is proudly in evidence. In the *Nicomachean Ethics*, Aristotle reports the Greek version of this view, though he does not accept it. Aristotle says,

> Now those activities are desirable in themselves from which nothing is sought beyond the activity. And of this nature virtuous actions are thought to be; for to do noble and good deeds is a thing desirable for its own sake.[16]

Only philosophical endeavor, in Aristotle's opinion, satisfies the criterion of being desirable in itself. But it is obvious that some in Greece thought otherwise. One might mention the love of great political deeds done for one's country that informs the speeches of Pericles in Thucydides' *The Peloponnesian War*. Machiavelli's great model turns out to be the civic spirit of republican Rome which he wishes revived in his native Florence. Virtue is not epitomized by philosophical wisdom. It certainly is radically different from Christian virtue, the virtue of humility, forbearance, and otherworldliness. Machiavelli's virtù is manliness, courage, and the willingness to love one's country more than one's own soul. Of course, the virtù of the citizenry in the good republic has an aim: it is to be employed in the service of the freedom and greatness of one's city. There is no private value that begins to compare to the moral value inherent in the freedom and greatness of one's city. Implicit, however, in Machiavelli's writing is the old Greek and Roman sense that political deeds are to be prized not only for their utility to the city, but also for the way in which they express virility, in the most extended meaning of that word. The preservation of one's city as a healthy republic is at the same time the

---

[16] Aristotle, *Nicomachean Ethics* (X, 6), in Richard McKeon, *op. cit.*, p. 1102.

preservation of the stage on which the forms of virility are best manifested. Politics and war are man's true vocation. Adventure is his happiness.

We have said that the key to the maximal conception of the common good found in Plato, Aristotle, Machiavelli, Rousseau, and Hegel is the view taken of the value of public things as opposed to private things. All these theorists find in public things, when they are as they are supposed to be, a worth that transcends normal, everyday private things, as it transcends the more ambitious strivings of private life. Without such an estimation, the maximal conception of the common good, the maximal expectation held out for the net workings of the political system, would not be held. The political pattern (in the case of Plato and Hegel) and the political process (in the case of Aristotle, Machiavelli, and Rousseau) would not be charged with so much moral greatness. The sense that politics matters not only for the private and social ends of life it protects but for the supreme universal principle it reflects (in the case of Plato and Hegel) or the virtuous activity peculiar to it (in the case of Aristotle, Machiavelli, and Rousseau) would not be so centrally present. We must now mention the role played by these writers' other notions in support of their view of politics. To repeat, the influential notions deal with human nature, the material conditions of life, and the value of all worldly things as opposed to spiritual things.

In regard to human nature, all five theorists have an extremely pessimistic view. Their recital of the recurring features of human experience is full of woe at the tendency of men to be driven by passion, appetite, and self-seeking. Plato, Aristotle, and Rousseau, however, present the classic case for the belief that under the proper conditions human nature can be redeemed. Their faith in education is famous, and by "education" is meant not only formal schooling but the force of the whole social environment. Much of Plato's *Republic* (and many of his other writings), some of Aristotle's *Politics*, and some of Rousseau's *The Social Contract* (together with his *Emile*) are devoted to a discussion of what is needed thoroughly to remake character. Which is to say that though these three writers are appalled by the spectacle of human behavior, they do not believe in the incorrigibility of human nature. Rousseau explicitly denounces the Christian doctrine of original sin. To be sure, Plato, in the very last part of *The Republic* (the myth of Er), beautifully suggests that education could never really touch the deepest reaches of the character of any but a few. Nevertheless, even Plato takes with utmost seriousness the project of human redemption.

In contrast, Machiavelli and Hegel rest content with the regulation of the stuff of ordinary human nature. Both attribute to the people a capacity to be intensely loyal to their native countries, and see in this loyalty the basis of the projected political orders. Once loyalty is assured, the interests and desires of men remain substantially intact, subject to the restrictions and compromises needed to insure the survival of everyone in society. For both men, patriotism will engage the energies of men and supply a splendid way of directing those energies outward, rather than having them tear society apart in civil and class war. No one has spoken more cynically of human nature than Machiavelli. His major purpose, however, is not to cure human nature of its wickedness, but to employ that wickedness in a cause (the freedom and greatness of the state) in a manner that is as little destructive domestically as possible. In any case, the life of political action is unthinkable without the human drives pious moralists condemn. The point is to guide those drives into the right channel.

Thus all five theorists work hard to show that they have reckoned with human nature in their visions of the right order of politics. They are eager to exploit different segments of the spectrum of human nature. But all are sure that in suitable circumstances their theories will not be betrayed by human frailty. The extremism of their moral claims on the political order could not otherwise be sustained.

There is one specific aspect of human nature that must be referred to: human inequality. These five theorists can be divided into two groups, with Plato, Aristotle, and Hegel affirming the decisive political significance of human inequality, and Machiavelli and Rousseau, with comparable intensity, founding their political systems on a belief in human equality. What is involved is a calculation concerning the distribution of political capacity among men. As is well known, Plato's *Republic* can exist only if philosophers rule, only if those in possession of metaphysical wisdom alone rule, and rule absolutely. To become a philosopher, a man must undergo the most arduous discipline of his desires, his manly aggressiveness, and his moral and intellectual faculties. Only then can a man be trusted with total political domination over a society. And if there is such a man, or if there are a few such men, then his (or their) total political domination will realize the pattern of political perfection, with all the blessings for all the people attendant on such an arrangement. But Plato insists that only a tiny fraction of any group of people could possibly have the native endowment, the gold in their souls, adequate to the enterprise of ultimate refinement: the transformation of a man into a philosopher. It is the measure of Plato's optimism that he thinks at least a few can be trusted with absolute power, while also thinking that power ordinarily corrupts him who wields any degree of it.

The doctrine of human inequality takes a racialist form in Aristotle. It is Aristotle's belief that all and only Greeks have the native endowment necessary to lead the life of virtue. In the ideal political society, labor is confined to a subject foreign population, who are incapable, by nature, of the life of virtue. The beneficiaries of this labor are the class of citizens—and only Greeks have it in them to be worthy of citizenship. Leisure for the citizens is made possible by the labor of the inferior classes. Without leisure, the cultivation of the citizenry, as Aristotle envisages that cultivation, cannot take place. Leisure is required for virtue; only the virtuous deserve citizenship; all citizens will be virtuous. The ideal society is, by definition, that society in which all social institutions promote the life of virtue, and which restricts citizenship to the virtuous. The virtuous life, in its moral and intellectual fullness, is the only life of human happiness. (It may be noted that not until the racist doctrines of the nineteenth and twentieth centuries have the political implications of a claimed human inequality been as drastically pursued as Plato and Aristotle pursued them.)

Hegel does not essay a theory of human equality. He simply assumes that in the good society, men will live in all sorts of conditions, with varying levels of moral and intellectual development. The division of labor will take the form of a class-stratified society. Unlike Plato, he does not seek to adjust the division of labor to innate human capacities. Hegel makes it clear, however, that only the ruling circles will have a genuinely rational understanding of the true world-historical meaning of the projected political order, and will have, besides, the political knowledge and talent requisite to rule in a constitutional monarchy. "Public opinion"— the common mind of the great mass of people—will be the repository of both common sense and the eternal principles of justice. But

> Public opinion . . . deserves to be as much respected as despised— despised for its concrete expression and for the concrete consciousness it expresses, respected for its essential basis, a basis which only glimmers more or less dimly in that concrete expression. But in itself it has no criterion of discrimination, nor has it the ability to extract the substantive element it contains and raise it to precise knowledge. Thus to be independent of public opinion is the first formal condition of achieving anything great or rational whether in life or science.[17]

The people are wiser than they know, and live their wisdom.

Machiavelli also assumes the existence of social classes in the good republic. Indeed, he assumes the existence of a hereditary nobility as one of the classes. This does not commit him, however, to the view that the nobility should monopolize political power. The people will share in power; they will share in the moral responsibilities and opportunities which only the life of free citizenship grants to men. Unkind though Machiavelli is to human nature (to engage in understatement), he has a number of kind things to say about "the people," the commoners. He

---

[17] Hegel, *op. cit.*, p. 205.

trusts to their good sense and their energy; he finds that they pose much less of a threat to the established order and are far less acquisitive or rapacious than those at the top of the social order. He says, in the *Discourses:*

> The demands of a free people are rarely pernicious to their liberty; they are generally inspired by oppressions, experienced or apprehended; and if their fears are ill founded, resort is had to public assemblies where the mere eloquence of a single good and respectable man will make them sensible of their error.[18]

Neither Platonic wisdom nor Aristotelian virtue is needed to take part in political life. All that is needed is what almost all men who live in an uncorrupted political society are certain to have.

Rousseau's adherence to the doctrine of human equality is the prime feature of his moral sense of the world. His early and brilliant essay *A Discourse on the Origin of Inequality* (1755) retells the history of man as one long story of falling away from the primitive condition of human equality. Every step in the direction of human cooperation, inventive skill and technological advance, and social order is simultaneously a step away from the purity and simplicity of the original human situation of isolated and unpredatory independence. The ultimate sin against equality is the complexity of high civilization, for high civilization is the most fully realized inequality. Different classes of men are different men: genuine communication between them is impossible. Classes also signify exploitation. Those at the top live in a vain artificiality; those at the bottom in an unrelieved brutality. The common human nature is buried under the weight of repressive laws, habits, and manners. The good society, which is described in *The Social Contract*, is precisely that society which seeks to restore men to a condition of equality. Only now the equality can no longer be natural; it must be social and moral. The new equality is the equality of free citizens, equal before the law, equal in their participation in making the law, roughly equal in their material possessions, equal in the benefits they gain from living together, equal in the sacrifices they must make to preserve their society. And they are similar in their style of life. The channels of human communication are reopened. The innate human potentiality for goodness is made actual. Citizenship does not require intellectual sophistication or philosophical discipline. It needs common sense, a good heart, and a lively awareness of advantage. These things men will have, once they are raised and live in a society appropriate to their potentiality.

---

[18] Niccolò Machiavelli, *Discourses on the First Ten Books of Titus Livius* (I, 9), in Niccolò Machiavelli, *The Prince and the Discourses,* trans. Christian E. Detmold (New York: The Modern Library, 1940), p. 120.

In comparison with the worth placed on public as opposed to private things, and in the judgment passed on human nature, the two other factors generally influencing a theorist's expectations regarding the political system are of minor importance here. We should, nevertheless, give some attention to them. As will be recalled, these factors are the assumptions made about the material conditions of life, and the worth of worldly as opposed to spiritual things.

If public life, either as a pattern or as a process, is accorded primacy, material resources will be seen in the light of their adequacy to sustain public life, rather than in the light of their adequacy to provide as much satisfaction as possible for private individuals and groups. If the theorist hypothesizes dire scarcity and thinks that the most efficient or unscrupulous use of resources still will not allay the appetites of enough people, then he cannot imagine that his intended political order will hold very much moral promise. If life is a constant struggle with scarcity, public life cannot easily be accorded primacy. It turns out that Plato, Aristotle, Machiavelli, and Rousseau assume something better than scarcity; they assume a decent sufficiency. On the other hand, Hegel says,

> It . . . becomes apparent that despite an excess of wealth civil society is not rich enough, i.e., its own resources are insufficient to check excessive poverty and the creation of a penurious rabble.[19]

But this lack drives the nation "beyond its limits": it seeks markets and presumably will engage in war to solve its domestic problems.[20] Such manifestations of the will and power of the state are, however, the kinds of political assertion which Hegel saw as the essence of the state. Scarcity, in this case, thus becomes integral to the political pattern he envisages.

It is a further fact that the political ideals of Plato, Aristotle, Machiavelli, and Rousseau are facilitated by moderation in material goods, and would in fact be threatened by anything resembling luxury. The material basis of their good societies should not therefore be too advanced. Plato's ruling class lives in the utmost collective simplicity, while the mass of people, though retaining private property and enjoying the pleasures ordinary men must be allowed to enjoy, are expected to be generally temperate. Aristotle firmly believes that virtue is compatible only with moderate possessions: leisure, not wealth, is the desideratum. The pursuit of wealth debases the character. Machiavelli, in giving advice to the founders of cities, is tempted to say that the site should be a sterile country because

> virtue has more sway where labor is the result of necessity rather than of choice . . . the people, compelled by necessity to be indus-

---

[19] Hegel, op. cit., p. 150.
[20] Ibid., p. 151.

trious, and therefore less given to idleness, would be more united, and less exposed by the poverty of the country to occasions for discord.[21]

But security requires power; power requires the avoidance of impover-ished circumstances. The founder must choose a fertile spot, but insure against the perils of plenty by wise customs, strict discipline, and severe exercises. In any case, Machiavelli's notion of material sufficiency apparently seems to him easy of fulfillment. It would have been meager by modern standards. Rousseau greatly fears the moral effects of luxury. He wants the economic system of the good society to be as simple and as spare as possible. He wishes to avoid economic classes, conflicts of interest, the presence of avarice and envy, the forgetfulness of public duty in preoccupation with getting and spending. The agrarian way of life will be the nurse of virtuous citizenship.

It becomes clear that the political vision of none of those who make the most extreme moral claims on the political system is impeded by economic considerations. When they define perfection, the gratification of the senses has only a small place.

The last factor we see as influential in determining the level of a theorist's political expectations, namely, the value of worldly as opposed to spiritual things, can be quickly treated. We have already seen that within the class of all worldly things, public things far surpass private things in worth. Is there some kind of spiritual or contemplative activity that, in turn, far surpasses public things? The answer for Plato and Aristotle is unmistakable. The life of contemplation, the life dedicated to the attainment of knowledge of the source and nature of being, is the best possible life for those capable of it. Plato's parable of the Cave, at the beginning of Book VII of *The Republic,* is the most powerful statement of this position in the literature of the world. Plato makes it clear that the philosopher takes on the burden of politics with the greatest reluctance, and does so to avoid the selfish or incompetent rule of the unphilosophical. Aristotle speaks of the contemplative life as an imitation of God. On the other hand, Machiavelli seems fairly indifferent to the contemplative life, and Rousseau hostile to most of the forms it takes.[22] Refinement of mind precludes a wholehearted civic virtue. Even more, both writers judge religion by the standard of its efficacy in uniting the people and increasing their devotion to the interests of society (though Rousseau says he believes that the efficacious religion is also the true one). Hegel's position is ambiguous. Some in the Hegelian tradition, like

---

[21] Machiavelli, *op. cit.* (I, 1), p. 107.
[22] Rousseau, "A Discourse on the Moral Effects of the Arts and Sciences," in Rousseau, *op. cit.,* pp. 151–156.

F. H. Bradley in *Ethical Studies,* posit values higher than any that are political. Bradley says,

> It is a moral duty for the artist or the inquirer to lead the life of one, and a moral offence when he fails to do so. But on the other hand it is impossible, without violent straining of the facts, to turn these virtues into social virtues or duties to my neighbour. . . . The end they aim at is a single end of their own, the content of which does not necessarily involve the good of other men.[23]

The good self contains aspects not exhausted by "my station and its duties," by one's contribution to the putatively perfect pattern of political and social relations.

We thus conclude our consideration of the three main categories into which the leading political theorists in the West can be placed. We have certainly not discussed all the theorists, and we do not claim more for the categories than that they are a useful way of coming to terms with the great variety of political theory. At the same time, we have proposed an explanation (or elements of an explanation) for that variety.

The Inevitability of Disagreement in Political Theory

We must now return to the five approaches to the variety of political theory already noticed earlier. These approaches were the esthetic, the relativist, the plausible, the dogmatic, and the eclectic. Our objection to these approaches was that they all failed to acknowledge the continuous commitment made by political theorists to the idea of the common good. The universal habit is to search for that political value or principle which qualifies as the highest end toward which political societies ought to aspire. What is the most valuable end for all men living in a society that the institutions of government can be entrusted to achieve? What is it, within the reach of the political process, that conduces most to human happiness? Or if happiness is not a word that can cover all the conditions of life which political theorists hope will result if the diverse ends they advocate are attained, then the question can be put as follows, What is it, within the reach of the political process, that conduces to the mode of existence that men are properly supposed to follow? All political theorists keep in mind this question, in one or another of its forms. They would not think they were discharging their responsibility as political theorists if they did not.

Despite this unanimity, it is nevertheless patently obvious that political theorists have, in fact, entered into serious disagreement with each other. We have tried to suggest that the source of disagreement is to be found primarily in the background of the theorist's thought. This back-

---

[23] F. H. Bradley, *Ethical Studies* (2nd ed., Oxford: Clarendon Press, 1927), p. 223.

ground is made up of ideas concerning human nature, the material basis of life, the value of worldly things as opposed to spiritual or contemplative things, and the value of private things as opposed to public things. Disagreement on these matters will lead to disagreement on the common good. The question then becomes, Must men disagree on the matters that make up the background of their thought? Or is some reconciliation or resolution possible? If the answer is no, then we must also say that men will always disagree about the common good.

The brief answer is that no reconciliation or resolution is possible. The background of a writer's political theory constitutes problematic elements about which thoughtful and well-intentioned men will inevitably hold contrasting, even contradictory, opinions. In the words of John Plamenatz:

> These theories are more than attempts to explain society and government, and more also than apologies for or attacks upon the established order. They are philosophies of life. . . . All these theories, no matter how "pretentious" or "modest" they may be, are elaborate philosophies which contain a large element which is not science or conceptual analysis or ideology in the Marxian sense. They are what I venture to call, for want of a better word, practical philosophies or philosophies of man.[24]

It is inconceivable that all thoughtful and well-intentioned men should hold the same, or roughly the same, philosophy of life. If we look at nothing more than those portions of it which we have singled out as decisive in the formulation of a political theory, we will see that contention about them is only to be expected. They do involve, to some degree, looking at the facts. And doubtless to that degree, persistent inquiry could establish the facts, and men would cease to have a warrant to disagree. But how much inconclusiveness would such inquiry remedy? How important are the facts to views on human nature, the material basis of life, the value of spiritual and contemplative things as opposed to worldly things, the value of public as opposed to private things?

It must be granted that on the question of the material basis of life the factual component is very large. At any given time, some reasonable assumptions could be made about the present economic capacities of the real world, and about the limits set by those capacities on any but the most utopian conjectures. Even on this subject, however, equally serious men could entertain widely divergent hopes in regard to possible alternative methods of production and distribution. The most ambitious economic science—and such a science is a comparatively late development—could not interpose itself between a speculative political theorist

---

[24] John Plamenatz, *Man and Society* (2 vols., New York: McGraw-Hill Book Company, 1963), vol. I, pp. xiv–xv.

and some fond scheme of the good society. Furthermore, as we have seen, even those theorists who expect the most from the political system do not incorporate the expectation of abundance into their idealism. At least until the middle of the nineteenth century, political theorists were content to remain within a narrow range of economic possibility. But much variation is permissible within that range. We could not expect all observers to arrive at identical conclusions concerning the appropriate economic arrangements. Beyond a condition of primitivity or bleak scarcity, anyone who was sensitive to economic problems, and who wished to construct a political theory, would wish to explore material potentialities not reached, or reached only imperfectly, in the world around him. This kind of exploration must perforce be in different directions. Uncertainty of knowledge encourages the imagination and allows the emergence of various responses, even as the effort to know and the application of commonly acceptable methods of argument circumscribe the imagination and limit the number of responses meant to be taken seriously.

Similarly in the matter of human nature, men's imaginations are free, within quite wide margins, to paint numerous pictures of mankind. Who could ever hope to take the pictures of the great moralists, the great poets and novelists, the great psychologists, and the great political theorists and make them into one picture? The only views of human nature ruled out are the grossly simple or caricatured ones. The student looks for sharp insight into the human personality, for subtlety of perception, for awareness of incorrigible opacity. When generalizations are made, we must feel them to be earned. And we are not allowed to see them as eternally or unqualifiedly true. Any trace of easy cynicism or glib optimism, pious hopefulness or a willful reveling in the sordid is repellent, and seems fraudulent. Once we exclude such views, many others remain. And despite the fact that observers of human nature share beliefs about human nature with each other, a compelling view will have ingredients of its own. It is not so much that a great view will contain discoveries, although now and then we are inclined to think that something new about human nature has at last been said. Rather, familiar aspects of human nature will be given new emphasis, new patterns of familiar motives will be disclosed, familiar facts will be unburdened of hitherto hidden implications, familiar human purposes, responses, and characteristics will be given forceful new dramatization and illustration.

Every view of human nature is necessarily incomplete; it is also necessarily more attentive to some aspects than to others, no matter how comprehensive it tries to be. There is too much for any one thinker, or tradition of thinkers to know it, profound though he or they may be. The attempt to piece together the whole truth from a multiplicity of sources can result in nothing but chaos.

For all these reasons, agreement on human nature can never be reached. Every political thinker, armed with only a part of the truth and certain to be led into error some of the time, will look at man in a somewhat different way from any other political thinker. The consequences for political theory are apparent: contrasting views of human nature, in combination with contrasting views of other subjects, will produce varieties of political theory. There is no omniscient source to appeal to. Disagreement on great political issues as well as minor ones is altogether expectable.

Assessments of worldly things in relation to spiritual things and of private things in relation to public things partakes of the same indeterminacy as judgments about the material basis of social life and the capacities and weaknesses of human nature. Such assessments are dependent on a writer's ultimate conception of what man should be, of what human goodness, greatness, or perfection consists in, of the sources of human happiness, of the activities that best comport with human dignity or excellence, of what is peculiarly or appropriately human. In turn, this conception may be dependent on a religious or metaphysical understanding, or perhaps on some purely secular, even antimetaphysical, understanding. No political theorist is innocent of such large notions, even though they are not always spelled out or carefully connected to his political theory. In any case, adjudication between competing world views (in the most extended sense) is a hopeless venture. The role of facts is small and very ambiguous. The appeal to faith, intuition, or incommunicable knowledge is frequent. No one would wish to deny that discussion and argument are possible here; no one would wish to deny that some world views carry more conviction or are more free of perplexity than others. For periods of time, some world views appear to dominate, while others go out of fashion. Some elements of a world view are revived and blended with elements of other world views, while some elements are discarded, seemingly forever. Still, a man's mind does not rest: unanimity on a single world view is never reached. W. E. Kennick, speaking of metaphysical arguments, concludes,

> The first curious feature of metaphysics is the notorious fact . . . that its disputes have gone unresolved for over two thousand years in spite of the fact that some of the best minds of the race have labored at their solution . . . another [feature is] the prevalence in it of antinomies, contradictory conclusions that appear to be equally reasonable or necessary.[25]

[25] W. E. Kennick, "The Enigma of Metaphysics," in W. E. Kennick and Morris Lazerowitz (eds.), *Metaphysics: Readings and Reappraisals* (Englewood Cliffs, N.J.: Prentice-Hall, 1966), pp. 3, 10.

Is there a God? If so, does he have purposes? If so, does he have purposes for mankind? If so, what are they? How can they be found out? How can they be realized? Is there an afterlife? If so, how should that affect the way in which men live on earth? If there is no God, are there any consequences for morality? If there is no afterlife, are there any consequences for morality? Is nature informed by reason? If so, what is its relation to human purposes? If not, where shall man find his purposes? Does history have a meaning? Is there such a thing as inevitable progress? What makes men truly happy? How is man distinct from the rest of nature? Such questions and others like them continue to haunt thoughtful men. And as long as they do, moral speculation about politics will go on, and take divergent forms, and propound divergent theses.

With so much chance for contention over issues forming the background of political theory, there is small cause for wonder at the disagreement over the common good. But reference to background does not dispose of the subject of disagreement. It need not be vulgar to take into account the personality of the political theorist, and his experiences and social conditioning. The integrity of political theory is not damaged when the historian tells us about the temperament of a theorist or his political associations, the events he witnessed, and the interests toward which he was especially friendly, or when the historian tries to describe the factors shaping the thought of a period which those then alive were unconscious of, or did not examine or feel the necessity to specify. Intellectual effort does not have unconditioned autonomy. "The man and his times"—a phrase often used in accounts of a political theorist's work—must be studied, because some of the sources of political theory are found there. Hence part of the explanation of disagreemnt among political theorists is found there.

In sum, two points must be affirmed. First, political theory has always been dedicated to defining the common good, and thus to answering the question of what the end of government ought to be. Second, for the reasons we have taken up, a number of definitions have been traditionally given, despite the general commitment to the common good. Our dissatisfaction with the five approaches to explaining disagreement among political theorists derives from their failure to see the general commitment throughout all the disagreement, and from their attempt to account for the disagreement without reference to that commitment. Still, these approaches deserve another brief look.

Once the idea of the common good is insisted on, each of these approaches yields something of value. We have borrowed a good deal from them, as we have ventured to make sense of the history of political theory. These approaches are not completely at odds with each other. Acceptance of one does not cancel the rest. They may serve different uses; they certainly answer to different moods. Each of them holds clues for the exploitation of the riches of political theory. The point is to avoid the excesses inherent in them and to reject what is not compatible with the idea that the common good is the constant aspiration.

The esthetic approach brings out the heroism (though sometimes reckless) of the role of the political intellectual. Confronted with a subject that seems hopelessly complicated, except in rare moments of clarity and inspiration, the solitary writer undertakes a huge statement. Who could resist admiration for such effort? The excess of the esthetic approach is to disregard the simple matter that the history of political theory is not the record of men trying to impress with their prowess or create beautiful structures of thought for our idle examination. Political theorists are, above all, trying to instruct those who read them and to give them moral elucidation. Their aim is moral truth; their hope is sometimes to defend, more often to criticize and improve, and sometimes to change the world over. The deadly seriousness of politics is imparted by most political theorists. It is fine if the works of political theory give pleasure. But that is not their intention, nor is it their largest value. The esthetic approach is too precious.

The relativist approach is for us probably the easiest of all to which to succumb because it fits in so neatly with the hyper-developed historical sense that has marked much of Western thought since the time of Hegel. Marxism has done much to persuade even non-Marxists of the near-enslavement of thought, especially political and social thought, to place and time, to need and interest. The reduction of such thought to "ideology" or to "myth" has proceeded under the influence of Marxism. Then, too, the critique of nonscientific language by the logical positivists, in this century, has worked to rob many of the belief that moral discourse can be rational discourse. Where Marxists see political and social thought as an emanation of definite class interests in specific historical circumstances, positivists see this thought as an emanation from the tastes and feelings of the individual. Where the Marxists deny the possibility of transcending the restrictions imposed on thought by the struggles of classes, the positivists deny that the language of morals has any meaning, but is, instead, the unrational and indefensible assertion of personal preference. We cannot enter here into a consideration of these complex doctrines. We can, however, register some qualified praise for the way in which Marxism has alerted thinkers and students of thought to the elements of hypocrisy and cynicism, habitual unawareness, illicit extension of relevance, anachronism, and changeable content of old words and concepts that are found in political theory. But that surely is not the whole story: these elements do not make up all that there is in any political theory.

The works of political theory that have survived the test of time, that continue to be read and pondered, are just those works that escape the confines which Marxism makes so much of. The great political theories may each possess ideological aspects or be put to ideological uses. They also, and more importantly, possess creative originality which cannot be accounted for by historical necessities. And they demonstrate the continuity of philosophical concerns, philosophical questions and problems, from generation to generation, from culture to culture. We have accorded great weight to the contribution made by background notions to the work of the political theorist. These notions are not the predictable secretions of any one time or place, but the perennial preoccupation of thoughtful men in their fascinated struggle with the meaning of life. No matter how much the economic systems of men have changed, they have continued to philosophize in much the same manner as the first philosophers. We cannot deny that the advent of industrial technology, with its unprecedented promise of abundance and leisure, has added a novel quantity to men's political speculation. But the connection between abundance and speculation is not uniform or simple, and it does not destroy the links between the political thought of the past century and all the political thought of earlier times. All relativist critiques of the history of political theory run the grave risk of presuming that they can obliterate rationality. (About positivism, it is better to say nothing than to say little, though it too suffers from the same debilitating crudity as Marxism and other relativisms.)

The plausibility approach has the merit of locating the sources of political theory in premises that are not themselves political. We have tried to do just that in this essay. The difficulty with this approach is that it converts these premises into purely factual ones. In contrast, we have tried to suggest that the place of facts in views of the material basis of life, human nature, the value of worldly things, and the value of public things is limited. It is a rare background notion that would now commonly be thought refuted. Plato's theory of incommunicable metaphysical wisdom, Aristotle's theory of the innate inferiority of non-Greek races, the Stoic theory of the mind of the universe, the Augustinian doctrine of predestination, the Hegelian theory of historical stages, all may now have ceased to command any but the slightest allegiance among philosophers. Still this fact does not render the political theories of Plato, Aristotle, and the others obsolete. Much remains alive in their works. And it would be too much to say that most analogous background notions have experienced the same kind of rejection. The plausibility approach tends to be too hasty.

The sanity of the dogmatic approach depends on the species of dogmatism. One can believe that correct moral understanding of political

ends is the property of only one political tradition, and yet be intellectually nourished by other traditions. One can have a moral commitment to
a political position, despite the temptation to yield to skepticism under
the pressure of moral disagreement and political complexity. One can be
certain that one has the truth, but allow that those in error have striven
for the truth. One can be grateful for the renewed life given one's firmest
principles by the contrast or competition with other principles. One can
sincerely feel that life is threatened by the spread of certain kinds of political ideas, but not indulge in fantasies of censorship. All this is a sane
dogmatism. Every man who takes politics seriously will have his dogmatism, even if it be merely the dogmatism of uncertainty. The most
liberal, most democratic, most tolerant man must sooner or later subscribe to some settled principles or to some view of the good man, the
good life, or the good society. Otherwise, he could be said to have no
political position at all.

Let us concede all the foregoing arguments to what we have abstract-
ly called the dogmatic approach. We then are entitled to go on to say
that there are also unbalanced or fanatical dogmatisms which cast a
terrible blight on the whole enterprise of moral speculation about politics.
One need not be a crude relativist to permit one's sense of human variety
to lead to generosity in appraising the efforts of those thought deeply
wrong. Granted that there are some scandalous moments in the history of
political theory: Aristotle's advice to tyrants in Book V of the *Politics*,
or his defense of slavery; some of Machiavelli's advice to the Prince;
Hegel's intolerable adoration of the state. (Let us leave aside ideologies
mistaken for political theories, like Fascism, Nazi racism, much in Soviet
Marxism.) How much do these scandalous moments add up to? The pre-
ponderance of political theory is—though it may sound naive to say so
—pure in motivation. Naturally, good motives do not excuse bad acts. But
political theories held to be wrong, even harmful, are not to be likened
to bad acts. At most, one can say that the adversaries are misguided,
misinformed, or obtuse. Respect does not thereby have to lessen. Finally,
it *is* a question of respect. The dogmatic approach, in its extreme forms,
is disrespectful.

Of all the approaches, the most congenial to a man with liberal-
democratic sympathies is the eclectic. It is obviously a version of the
intellectual procedure advocated by Mill in *On Liberty*. Its main fault
is that, despite the willingness of those who hold it to learn from any
source that has something to teach, it may ignore the fact that all the
great political theories are equally devoted to the search for the common
good. Many of the truths an eclecticist extracts (from theories which he
mostly rejects) are the fruits of men who were not themselves eclectic,
and who discovered what they did only because they were committed to

a line of thought that was often narrow, exclusive, and deliberately inhospitable to large areas of experience. In his essay on *Bentham*, Mill himself supplies a check on too eager an eclecticism:

> For our own part, we have a large tolerance for one-eyed men, provided their one eye is a penetrating one: if they saw more, they probably would not see so keenly, nor so eagerly pursue one course of inquiry. Almost all rich veins of original and striking speculation have been opened by systematic half-thinkers. . . .[26]

Mill goes on to voice his hope that "complete thinkers" will correct the work of strongly partial philosophers. But one is left wondering whether the desire for completeness will not result in yet another incompleteness, or result, alternatively, in a confused mixture of hopelessly incompatible ingredients. Eclecticism may unfortunately tend to be parasitic. The liberal democrat may not wish to fancy himself a dogmatist. He must, however, acknowledge the irremovable differences between his views and the views found in other political theories, even while he bestows due respect on his adversaries.

---

[26] John Stuart Mill, "Bentham," in Marshall Cohen (ed.), *The Philosophy of John Stuart Mill* (New York: The Modern Library, 1961), p. 25.

Chapter III

THE DISCUSSION OF MEANS
IN POLITICAL THEORY

It should be apparent, from what we have said so far, that the moral recommendations concerning the common good made by political theorists are embedded in extensive philosophizing about the moral life. When a definition—or conception—of the common good is put forth, the theorist is not content with merely stating a preference, and with hoping that his audience will accept his word for its correctness. Whatever one may think of the quality of the reasoning involved, or whatever one may think the proper mode of moral reasoning to be, political theorists characteristically try to demonstrate, to give support to, their recommendations. They feel they must merit credence; they search for sources of authentication. More than that, they take a large view of their subject, and explore such related matters as they think appropriate. They often acknowledge, and in some detail, the opposing views of others. All this leads to saying that they arrive philosophically at their recommendations concerning ends: they are philosophers of the moral life from the perspective of politics. Each political theory contains, or contributes to, an image of man.

Similarly, when political theorists make their recommendations concerning political institutions—the means fit for the envisaged ends—they also characteristically philosophize or theorize about political practice. They confront the deeply perplexing mass of political phenomena and try to give them some order. To repeat, their institutional recommendations are general in nature; they deal inclusively with most or all of the aspects of political practice; they offer a model of the ideal political system. But because they proceed philosophically in order to substantiate their recommendations, to support their models, one could say, as we already have, that each political theory contains, or contributes to, a sense of politics as a whole.

Philosophizing about Political Practice

What then does it mean to philosophize about political practice? A number of intellectual tasks figure in the history of political theory, as they still figure in the work of contemporary political scientists. (We must notice that philosophizing about the moral life from a political perspective is intertwined with philosophizing about political practice. It is usually hard to make a clear-cut distinction between the two kinds of philosophizing: they are often served by the same passages or arguments in a political theory.) First, many political theorists have tried to define the peculiar traits of political phenomena. What makes a situation or a relation political? What establishes the claim that government or public authority is qualitatively different from all other institutions and organizations in society? What is it about the human condition that makes politics in the abstract necessary? Should the essence of government be seen as the right to compel obedience by force or threat of force to certain general rules, or should it be seen as the greatest agency of rational cooperation in matters concerning the interests of all those who make up a society? Of all the other organizations and institutions in a society, which are those that can be said to work toward the same purposes as government, even though they may use other methods than the ones used by government? Does it show too narrow a sense of politics to confine politics to the processes of public authority, and omit study of other human institutions and organizations in which "political" relations exist—relations of command, control, manipulation, conflict—and in which "political" devices are employed—cunning, compromise, loyalty, charisma, bribery, persuasion, mystery?

Many political theorists have tried to clarify the meaning of significant concepts utilized by those who study politics and those who take part in political life. We have already made much of the attention given, in each case, to the concept held to define the content of the common good. But a political theory is not equivalent to the elaboration of one concept. To say that works of political theory are inclusive is to say, at the same time, that they will necessarily contain analysis of many political concepts. Indeed, any political argument, even the least formal, is bound to make reference to a number of concepts, to a number of words that occupy a prominent place in political discourse and that seem to have their most important uses in political discourse. Among the familiar concepts are the state, sovereignty, power, authority, influence, freedom, equality, order, justice, fairness, welfare, slavery, citizenship, obligation, rights, duties, consent, and law. To these may be added the names of forms of government such as tyranny, democracy, constitutional government, dictatorship, and so on.

It may be thought that a dictionary would suffice to give the meaning of these words: why do political theorists think that conceptual analysis is one of their main duties? One reason is that many of the most frequently recurrent political concepts are notoriously changeable. For centuries the same words have appeared and reappeared in political writing. These words have a history; they drop and pick up various associations. Conscious of that, political theorists often think they are obliged to detach themselves from earlier associations, to state exactly what they mean by a word. Another reason is that in any given time, a single word will have many uses, will find its way into all sorts of contexts, and will suffer from careless or imprecise handling. The requirement of clarity will thus supply the political theorist with an incentive to dwell on the meanings of crucial words, to give illustrations, to coax out of these words their implications. Then too many of these words are not always easy to manage: is X really a state, is act Y really a free one, does the principle of equality really entail practice Z? The common political words are abstractions and, despite a core of fairly routine application, are not amenable, after a certain point, to uncontestable usage. Next, the connections of concepts to each other must be treated. What is the relation between rights and duties, freedom and equality, justice and law? In the case of values, do they "fit into place in some single, interlocking, consistent, conceptual scheme"?[1] Which values derive from which, when there is derivation? If each value stands separately and is cherished independently, what happens when two or more values prove incompatible in practice after a certain point? What is the principle of reconciliation between them?

Last, many political concepts are invested with a fierce moral passion: men want to be able to say that others are wrong in their understanding of, say, freedom or justice or democracy, while they are right. Men fight for the possession of these words, and for the extremely favorable, almost sacred, connotations these words have. Men have fought, fight still, and will continue to fight in order to impose on the world their idea, or their pretended idea, of the true meaning of freedom or justice or democracy. Political words have the ability to awe or to mesmerize;

---

[1] J. L. Austin, "A Plea for Excuses," in *Philosophical Papers* (Oxford: Clarendon Press, 1961), p. 151.

the struggle for their control is part of the struggle for the control of political life. It is no wonder that political theorists have wrestled with meanings: they have done so not only out of love of philosophical honesty, but also out of a desire to influence political reality. But to say this is not to accuse them of the wish to deceive: they are not propagandists or ideologues. It is only to acknowledge the simple psychological facts involved in the formation and reception of political argument.

Another species of philosophizing about political practice found in political theories is the effort to find the proper "framework" for the comprehension of politics. The word "framework" is, however, hypnotic in its effect. Perhaps "metaphor" would be a more accurate way to describe the aim, because the aim turns out to be a search for a provisionally useful distortion, an imaginative and fruitful simplification of a body of relations, processes, rule-governed activities, and constantly surprising and irregular movements so manifold and so elusive as to be *directly* unassimilable by even the best intelligence. What must a political system —even the most minimal, even the least acceptable—add up to? What are its constituent elements, and how are they joined together? What are the roles, the functions, the agencies? To what finally—and this is the point of suggesting the word "metaphor"—shall the political system be likened, so that we shall have a ready way of looking at politics?

Plato finds in the soul (or human personality) the best metaphor for political society. (He worked the metaphor both ways.) St. Augustine thinks that the state is more like a band of thieves than anything else. Medieval political thought is dominated by the metaphor of the organism. Machiavelli sees all politics as either a battle or an alliance between talent and luck. Hobbes conceives of political society as a latent or muted condition of the war of all against all, of men in ceaseless motion barely held together when the population imagines its ruler to be its rational personification. Locke envisages political society as a web of consent, explicit or tacit. Rousseau hopes that in the good society the political will will be as singlemindedly dedicated to the preservation of all as the individual will is to the preservation of the individual. Hegel insists that ideally, the state is a "rational organism," in which "each member, by maintaining itself in its own position, *eo ipso* maintains the others in theirs."[2] He correspondingly rejects the abstract conception of the electorate as an "agglomeration of atoms."[3] On the other hand, Bentham and Spencer reduce political society precisely to that "agglomeration of atoms," though they do not use the phrase. The metaphors of Burke are abundant and contradictory: sometimes political society is a joint-stock company; sometimes a family settlement; sometimes "a partnership in all

---

[2] G. W. F. Hegel, *Philosophy of Right*, trans. T. M. Knox (Oxford: Clarendon Press, 1942), p. 187.
[3] *Ibid.*, p. 202.

science; a partnership in all art; a partnership in every virtue, and in all perfection."[4] For Madison the best political society would be described as a stable system of mutual social and political checks, a system in which the vices of all are to be restrained by the weaknesses of each in regard to the rest. For Marx, the state is the agent of the economically dominant class, and nothing more—or, at least, nothing more than a parasitic excrescence. (We may notice that today an influential metaphor for the political system is derived from the theory of communications: political society as a continuous flow of "information" between the people and government.) Delusion is avoided if these metaphors are understood for what they are: metaphors, not total descriptions. They do what metaphors are supposed to do: awaken the mind, please the mind, connect seemingly unconnectable things, explain the unfamiliar by the familiar, compress a great deal of sense into a vivid picture, organize insight.

Some political theorists, in a related endeavor, have tried to find the *key* to politics. They are not content with merely isolating the elements of the good political system, or all political systems. Nor are they content with a metaphoric way of connecting these elements, nor with any manner of connecting them that appears to accord equal weight to each of them. They do not want something static; they do not assume equilibrium is normal. Rather, they desire to know what generally provides movement in political systems, what accounts for political change and for the social change which is inextricably joined with political change. The history of politics is the history of change, often violent change. Is there a pattern to that change? Do political systems follow each other in a regular sequence? Is the source of change always the same? The hope is to capture that quantity, that x, which will make it unimportant to worry about mastering every detail in the hopeless complexity of political phenomena. Details would be trivial, appearances would no longer deceive, intellectual order could be imposed, if the key were found.

Where Aristotle and Montesquieu almost delight in demonstrating the numerous sources of change, the numerous factors that produce instability, other political theorists have sought a conclusive and all-embracing answer. Plato thinks he has found the key in the tendency of ruling classes to abuse their power and carry their demands on the rest of society too far. The inevitable division of society into classes possessed of unequal power and wealth, but equally possessed of the passion to keep or get, is the stage on which the identity of the oppressors and the oppressed regularly changes. But the nature of the play remains the same. Aristotle (in his more abstract moments), Polybius, and Cicero also see in the war of classes the key to political change. A more mystical key is found by

---

[4] Edmund Burke, *Reflections on the Revolution in France* (London: J. M. Dent, 1955), pp. 31, 56, 93.

St. Augustine: the inscrutable will of God, which bestows eminence and disaster on peoples in a way no science could ever penetrate. But leaving that overreaching fact aside, St. Augustine locates the source of turmoil in the human passions: pride and the wish for glory at best; at worst, greed and the lust for domination. Insofar as other Christian moralists are specific in their diagnosis of political mutability, they point to human infirmity, Adam's bequest to his children, as an ever-potent progenitor: four of the seven deadly sins (anger, pride, envy, avarice), and a host of lesser sins suffice to account for the raging spectacle of political change.

In a more secular spirit, Hobbes (following Thucydides) stresses the importance of gain, safety, and honor as the motives that conduce to keeping men in motion in all spheres of life, but most centrally in the political sphere. In effect Hobbes says that if the student wants to know why men rebel, or contend with each other in less extreme fashions, he should look to these motives and see which of them fits the occasion. What Christians call sins, Hobbes and those who follow him call appetites or desires. In that large and ambitious intellectual enterprise, the philosophy of history, political change is explained on two levels (analogous to the levels in St. Augustine's thought). On the first level—and Hegel is the typical example—the needs and passions of men in a world of scarcity and opportunity drive men to make and unmake political societies. On the higher level, all the exertions of men can be seen as forming a pattern not intended by anyone, but which is implicit in history, and which constitutes the underlying rationality of the world. History is the working out of that rationality; and once complete, the entire past can be viewed as a series of stages, each of them necessary and each leading to the next and higher one, until the last is reached. For Hegel, history is the story of the development of freedom as it is embodied in institutions and in the moral response of thoughtful men to those institutions. In the last stage, there are perfect institutions, known to be perfect and fully accepted as perfect. Freedom is perfect obedience to perfect laws. The key to politics is thus the secret of history, and now the secret can be told. Some other philosophers of history, in their capacity as theorists of inevitable progress, display roughly the same form in their thought.

The most famous modern search for the key to politics is, of course, that of Marx and the Marxists. The great historical changes come about when new means of production emerge to disturb the established order: new wine cannot be poured into old skins. No established order has the economic institutions and, secondarily, the political, legal, and moral institutions able to permit the totally efficient operation of the new means of production. In time, the old skins burst, and the old order gives way in a revolutionary upheaval (or series of upheavals) in which the work of progress is done by the class associated with the new means of production. They take power and begin the almost insensible process of replacing the old institutions with the new ones. The new means of production must have their way, and class struggles provide their motor force. Marxism teaches that in times of stability, all the institutions of society unconsciously or semiconsciously cooperate with the means of production; in times of radical political change, the cause is to be found in the prior radical economic change. In sum, one could say that in the history of political theory, the key to politics is found in a theory of human motivation or a philosophy of history (which also includes a theory of human motivation).

Some political theorists have tried, as it were, to draw a map of the field of politics. The effort is to sort out and classify the various kinds of political systems, past and present. The principles of classification have differed, but the two traditional ones have been classification on the basis of the size of the ruling class in relation to the population, and classification on the basis of the nature of the ruling class. Does one man rule, or do a few or the many? Do the wellborn rule, or do the military, or the business classes, or the great mass of poor people? What combinations are possible that allow for a mixed state? Within each kind of government, what sorts of tendencies are likely? What do all kinds have in common, and wherein are they distinctive? What are the devices, the resources, the preconditions of each? Subsidiary efforts have also been carried out: various aspects of the political process or various kinds of abnormal or unusual political movement have been classified. Revolutions, political parties, types of leadership, types of citizenship, and other matters have been treated comparatively.

A few political theorists have tried to articulate a formal sociology of politics. (We referred to this fact in Chapter I.) They have tried to disclose the relationships between political institutions and the other major institutions of society. How do institutions cooperate with each other to achieve a common end? How do institutions work at cross-purposes, and thus impede each other, and, what is more, weaken or transform each other? Great sociologies constructed from a political point of view are found in Plato, Aristotle, Hobbes, Montesquieu, Rousseau, Burke, Tocqueville, and Hegel, among others.

Finally, a few political theorists have tried to work out the right principles of political study, to establish a methodology for political inquiry. In what does accuracy consist? What must be observed, and how must it be observed, if one is to be sure one is speaking the truth about a political problem, or about politics in general? Is there a qualitative difference between the procedures for the study of nature and those for the study of political and social man? Is the science of politics, if it is a science, equivalent to the science of psychology? This methodological interest, especially strong among the Greek political writers, resumes its hold on political theorists with Hobbes. After his time, it is a fairly constant subject for scrutiny.

These then are the main ways of philosophizing or theorizing about political practice, as they are found in the history of political theory. Relying on history and current affairs, exploiting their experience and knowledge, political theorists have tried to summarize and make coherent their general political understanding and to present to their readers what we have called a sense of politics as a whole. When the effort is made to stand back from the onrush of politics in order to grasp its recurrent structures and situations, to gain perspective on it, to approach it comparatively, to see whether there is anything timeless about it, to rescue its vocabulary from debased imprecision, the various aspects of philosophizing we have mentioned must be undertaken.

Philosophizing as Preparation for Governmental Recommendations

Now these aspects may be undertaken independently of any moral intention. In recent times, a number of political scientists have engaged in these intellectual enterprises in the spirit of scientific neutrality, in order to advance our knowledge of political reality. But in the case of the traditional political theorists, philosophizing about political practice is in the cause of moral purpose. To be sure, they have desired to instruct men in the complexities of politics; and aside from their moral purpose, the works of political theory can still be read for the light shed on the philosophical problems of political practice. The student of political theory, however, must see that the philosophizing that confronts him in the succession of political theories is meant to prepare the way for recommendations concerning political practice which each political theorist aims to make. The philosophizing provides a context for the recommendations, and helps to establish credibility for them by assuring the reader that the theorist has surveyed much and pondered much before hazarding a statement of his own preferences. The concluding words of Aristotle's *Nicomachean Ethics* (echoed in his *Politics*) gives an excellent expression of the spirit of this approach:

> First, then, if anything has been said well in detail by earlier thinkers, let us try to review it; then in the light of the constitutions we have collected let us study what sorts of influence preserve and destroy states, and what sorts preserve or destroy the particular kinds of constitution, and to what causes it is due that some are well and others ill administered. When these have been studied we shall perhaps be more likely to see with a comprehensive view, which constitution is best, and how each must be ordered, and what laws and customs it must use, if it is to be at its best.[5]

---

[5] Aristotle, *Nicomachean Ethics* (X, 9), trans. W. D. Ross, in Richard McKeon (ed.), *The Basic Works of Aristotle* (New York: Random House, 1941), p. 1112.

The clarity achieved by the theorist—and naturally the degrees of clarity differ from theorist to theorist—is also intended to facilitate the reader's acceptance of the theorist's view. It is not that the theorist defines and distinguishes arbitrarily so that his conclusions will wear the disguise of inevitability. Rather it is that the task of clarification is usually seen as essentially purgative: to clear the reader's mind of much of what he thinks he already knows about political processes and political words. Political theories are written with two kinds of people in mind: those who think they are in possession of truth, and those who are lost in confusion and uncertainty. The theorist must persuade the first and rescue the second. The struggle for clarity is indispensable for both missions.

We do not mean to imply that the philosophizing is invariably successful, either from the point of view of the theorist's own purposes, or from the point of view of neutral political science. Although the commonly read political theorists are almost all men of genius, that is hardly a guarantee of success in a subject as hard as politics. We must use some standard of success other than complete or absolute, a standard foreign to philosophizing in all its forms, no matter what the subject. We shall return to this matter in the last chapter.

Once the stage has been set, once the theorist has discharged his philosophical duties, the moral recommendations concerning political practice may follow. These recommendations, general and inclusive, when taken together compose a model of a political system, an abstract presentation of the main features of the network of political relations. If we survey the literature of political theory, we find the main features to be as follows:

1. A description of the powers which government must have, and of the scope of its activity, if it is to be capable of securing and promoting the common good, and carrying out all other tasks subsidiary and instrumental to the common good, and if it is to make its own contribution to other ends to which the common good itself may be instrumental.

2. A general *delimitation* of the scope of governmental power, with elaboration of the principles that impose restrictions on the powers of government.

3. A description of the form of the recommended government, its agencies, and their relations to each other, especially the legislative and executive agencies.

Recommendations concerning other aspects of political life are also found in the works of political theory. One example is procedures by which government will act and will undergo changes of personnel, especially procedures having to do with elections, the administration of public policies, and the operation of the legal system. Another is the extent of political rights or citizenship among the people in society, with special reference to the qualifications for holding office and for voting.

Yet another is the principle of legitimacy, or the psychological way in which the people should regard their government: is it their parent or their servant, should they generally view it with awe or with skepticism or with something in between, should they imagine it as based on their individual or collective consent or on a common-sense expediency or on some kind of religious or magical foundation?

Not all the works of political theory deal with all these aspects because one is or some are outside the conceptual orientation of the period or tradition in which the theorist works, or because the theorist tacitly assumes that one is or some of them are closed issues that stand in no need of discussion. But we can say that the three main features have regularly elicited recommendations from political theorists, whatever else may or may not be found. We must now see how the recommendations concerning ends (the varieties of the common good) are connected to the recommendations concerning means (the main features of political practices).

Recommendations Concerning Powers and Scope of Government

Rigorous and systematic thought about the powers of government is usually thought to start with the theorists of the nation-state in the early modern period in Europe. Bodin, Hobbes, and Locke, responding to the gradual and painful replacement of the feudal system by a more coherent and centralized organization of political power, taught men to think about the powers of government in the manner which they still more or less use today. This is not to say that the classical and feudal writers ignored the problem, or that they have nothing to teach the contemporary student. It is only to say that from the time of the sixteenth century the distinction between the government and the people has tended to dominate political speculation. Before that time (even when allowance is made for Roman imperial practice), the notion of government as a discrete institution, clearly defined and standing above and apart from the other institutions of society, was not as sharply articulated as it was to be later. The result is that the study of sovereignty is best begun with the writers of the late sixteenth and the seventeenth centuries.

Locke defines political power as "a Right of making laws with Penalties of Death, and consequently all less Penalties, for the Regulating and Preserving of Property, and of employing the force of the Community, in the Execution of such Laws, and in defence of the Commonwealth from Foreign Injury, and all this only for the Publick Good."[6] Working from Locke's definition, we may say (1) that the essence of government is certain kinds of regulation; (2) that all men in society are

---

[6] John Locke, *The Second Treatise of Government* (I, 3), in Peter Laslett (ed.), *John Locke, Two Treatises of Government* (Cambridge: Cambridge University Press, 1960), p. 286.

subject to such regulation; (3) that such regulation will be supported by the threat of force to deter men from disobedience, and the use of force to punish all those who do in fact disobey; and (4) that in society, government alone may legitimately use or threaten force, in order to secure obedience to its regulation. Without these four qualities domestic peace cannot be assured, as Hobbes in his stark way and Locke in his blander way try to show. It is clear that for us today little thought is needed to vindicate their position. The only modern alternative is a position which claims that under the right circumstances—in a radically reformed society —coercive regulation together with the existence of a single locus of legitimate force is unnecessary for the attainment of any end. Such a position is anarchism, and to the degree that it does not fly in the face of elementary good sense, it provides for ways of regulation that strike most observers as more coercive than those of government. These are the ways of vigilantism and *ad hoc* deliberations and actions, lacking precision, certainty, uniformity, and even justice. The difference between sin and crime nearly disappears: whim, impulse, and disgust generate a rough and spasmodic course of social policy. To reject anarchism is not to say that the only regulation any society needs or has is political. Manners, morals, role expectations, religious belief are also methods of shaping behavior, gaining assent and conformity, and inwardly transforming men in the desired directions. Families, neighborhoods, places of employment, public means of communication, schools, private groups and institutions of every kind practice those methods, consciously and unconsciously. The point is that to be successful, some kinds of regulation necessitate the threat or use of force and hence must be political. There must be a government to stand behind them.

But to insist on the indispensability of a central agency of regulation that may use force or the threat of force, that regulates for all men in society, and that monopolizes legitimate force is not to dispose of the matter of the powers of government. What has so far been outlined is the set of formal preconditions for social peace. It is obvious that disagreement can be expected on quality (1), the kinds of regulation which government should undertake, the specific powers it must have, if domestic peace is to be assured. Diversity of opinion can also be expected on the question of what specific powers government should have, if the common good is to be achieved, when the common good is held to be something more than the preservation of domestic peace. To say it again, except for the Augustinian tradition and for Hobbes, most political theorists look to government for more than the preservation of domestic peace: peace is the *sine qua non* of anything valuable, but it is itself not the highest thing of value within the competency of government. It is not the only moral standard by which to judge the performance of government.

On the question of the specific powers needed for the preservation of domestic peace, it is Hobbes who asks for the most. In theory there is nothing government is not entitled to do, and do with the support of threatened or employed force. But Hobbes does pick out what he regards as the crucial areas of life in which governmental regulation should be exercised. Apart from conducting foreign policy, the major work of government is to secure contented men in their lives and possessions from the assaults of the covetous and the indigent, the ambitious and the desperate. Ancillary to this work is the effort to maintain the compliance and awe of the people before government, the leviathan. To modern readers there is little to cause surprise in the powers claimed by Hobbes for legitimate government, except for two of tremendous importance: they are, first, that government should regulate opinion and, second, that government should regulate property. Hobbes's mature thought was, as the truthful commonplace has it, dominated by experience of the great English Civil War—dominated, that is, by painful experience of the absence of peace. He found especially in the dissemination of Puritan thought one of the major causes of the war. The conclusion he drew was that censorship, governmental scrutiny of universities, and governmental prescription of the articles of religious faith would help to avoid civil war in the future. He also feared the growth of any sizable concentration of private power, particularly economic power, and instructed government to keep an ever-watchful eye on corporations. In his view, one of the doctrines "that tendeth to the dissolution of a Common-wealth, is that every private man has an absolute propriety in his goods; such as excludeth the right of the soveraign."[7] Protection of property did not preclude regulation, especially in the form of taxation without consent.

It did not seem to occur to Hobbes that by asking for less, a government could be stronger, that a dynasty could last longer. He did not see that tolerance can be a mode of securing peace, and that in some circumstances popular consent to economic regulation can also conduce to peace. A less rigid monarchy could *perhaps* have spared itself the fate of Charles I. After the Restoration of 1660, the English crown did in fact change some of its ways, even though it took the *coup d'état* of 1688–89 to achieve a lasting settlement and permit England to change, and change greatly, without recourse to revolutionary violence.

The fight to restrain government in the realms of property and opinion was the real substance of much later constitutionalist, libertarian, and liberal political thought in England, Europe, and America. Spinoza (though not conventionally liberal), Locke, Paine, and Mill, to name only a few prominent thinkers, formulated a variety of moral and pragmatic arguments in behalf of freedom of opinion. In reference to Hobbes,

---

[7] Thomas Hobbes, *Leviathan,* ed. Michael Oakeshott (Oxford: Basil Blackwell, 1957), p. 213.

the important point is that regulation of opinion was not held to be necessary for domestic peace. Locke and Spencer and the bulk of common thought in between affirmed the sacredness of property, until Green, the Fabian socialists, Dewey, and the liberal-welfarist tradition grew appalled by the problem of poverty, and reinstated the regulation of property as one of the rightful powers of government. At the present time, there is no area of life except for opinion which government cannot enter to regulate, according to liberal-welfarist theory. Though the institution of private property is defended as morally and practically desirable, it still must endure interference that ranges from progressive taxation to the fixing of wages and prices. In liberal-socialist theory the very institution of private property comes under attack. Again, in reference to Hobbes, the important point is that regulation of property was not justified primarily on the grounds that without it the authority of government would be eroded and peace thus disturbed, but rather on compassionate grounds.

Once the common good is defined as something more than the preservation of domestic peace, the matter of the powers of government, the scope of governmental activity, becomes more complicated. The multiple conceptions of the common good must obviously lead to various views of the sort of powers government must have. Each conception requires instrumentalities appropriate to it, and though almost all powers will be found specified by more than one political theorist, there will be different degrees of emphasis and different composite patterns. It is not our aim to take up every theorist, list the powers he specifies, and try to show the connection between those powers and his conception of the common good. We must content ourselves with a summary approach.

One way of attempting such an approach is to divide political theories into two groups. The first group is made up of those theories which grant to legitimate governments, either on paper or in the real world, a more or less free hand. Very few areas of social life are ruled out in advance as unsuitable for governmental regulation and intervention, save for the affairs of church, Catholic or Protestant. And where the theorists do not indicate whether government may act in a given area, the reader who is familiar with the prevailing norms of the writer's time may infer that the writer would have sanctioned such action. (For example, Machiavelli pays little attention to the institution of property and its regulation when he projects his ideal republic in *The Discourses*, though he assumes the permanent existence of the rich and poor. It would seem right to suppose that Florentine practice, as Machiavelli knew it, was accepted by him as proper.) The conception of the common good may be minimal, moderate, or maximal, and the scope of governmental activity defended still be large. The second group is made up of those theories which advocate limited government. Care is taken to demonstrate the desirability of confining government's scope, of reducing its powers, as much as possible. Until the eighteenth century, which saw the rise of laissez-faire economics and the beginnings of the moral doctrine of individualism, all theorists except for Locke and some in the more radical Puritan tradition were in the first group. After the eighteenth century the division between the two groups became pronounced. The first group included a wide range of reactionary, conservative, statist, reformist, and radical thinkers, whereas the second group included those who, in one way or another, continued and modified the teachings of Locke and Paine (despite the profound alterations in social conditions that had taken place since the time of Locke and Paine) and those who took their lead from Bentham. The idea of limited government is really a brief historical interlude, nostalgia for which is bound to grow with the growth of governmental powers.

The writers in the first group entrust much to government because they feel that only by doing so can the common good, as each understands it, be attained. We can say that in general these factors and assumptions among others conduce to an advocacy of extended scope for government: the framework of the city-state, in which the line between public and private is blurred, the amount of social space, of the physical and psychological distance between people, is small and the sense of interlocking destinies among people is strong; the assumption that relations with other states will be constantly perilous; the assumption that scarcity is the normal condition of human life, and that the attitudes and passions it engenders require an ever watchful government; the assumption that society needs a great deal of conscious, rational, expert centralized direction if it is not to languish or disintegrate, and that the mass of common people do not have the time or talent or good will to supply that direction spontaneously, regularly, and without political inducement or coercion.

Plato, in defining the common good as the preservation of ideal order, makes all the preceding assumptions, and also takes for granted the framework of the city-state. Equally important, his order depends, more than any other political system, on *character*, especially the character of the ruling class. In his view, no aspect or detail of life is free of influence on the formation of character, on education in the fullest sense. The upshot is that no aspect or detail of life goes untended by the philosopher-kings. Aristotle, in defining the common good in the ideal society as the life of virtuous citizenship, shares Plato's view on the formation of character, and thus shares his concern that government address its attention to all things. Some of the same considerations apply to Cicero, and his conception of the common good as justice in the framework of the city-state republic. The order of St. Thomas Aquinas, with its regard for the maintenance of orthodox Christianity against heretics and infidels, and with its share of paternalism, requires a wide sphere for government.

And Aquinas is followed by Calvin in the name of Protestant Christianity. The absolutist and divine-right theory of kinship, espoused by James I of England, among others, is infused by a spirit of extreme paternalism—a mixture of high respect for those who rule and considerable condescension for the multitude—and leads to an enormous principled grant of powers to the state. It is no accident that by reviving the definition of the common good as the life of virtuous citizenship, Rousseau defends political practices that confer a wide scope on both the sovereign people in their capacity as lawmakers and the executive or administrative agency. Though fanatic in his attachment of the principle of property and in his opposition to governmental measures to lessen poverty, Burke nevertheless bases the retention of his ideal order on extensive political supervision. In his concern for the greatness of the nation, Hegel finds many sources of domestic disturbance that threaten a glorious foreign policy and that therefore require governmental attention (such as scarcity). From the same concern there derives a commitment to social efficiency, which only an active government can insure.

When attacks on the teachings of those in the first group have been launched, the above assumptions which conduce to an advocacy of extended scope for government have been rejected as false, or if accepted as true still have not dissuaded theorists from championing limited government. Locke and Paine define the common good as the preservation of individual rights. Paine speaks of "security [as] the true design and end of government."[8] But both writers profess a belief in the sufficient rationality of most men. If not oppressed by government or driven to desperation by necessity, men will mind their business and will need government only for protection against the outside world and against those few "degenerates" (in Locke's term) who seek to take what is not their own. Paine expresses this optimistic view most passionately:

> Great part of that order which reigns among mankind is not the effect of government. It has its origin in the principles of society and the natural constitution of man. It existed prior to government, and would exist if the formality of government was abolished. The more perfect civilization is, the less occasion has it for government, because the more does it regulate its own affairs, and govern itself . . . Man . . . is more a creature of consistency than he is aware, or than governments would wish him to believe.[9]

He points to the experience of the American colonies, some of which had no established authority for a time after the Declaration of Independence,

---

[8] Thomas Paine, *Common Sense,* in Harry Hayden Clark (ed.), *Thomas Paine, Representative Selections* (New York: Hill and Wang, 1961), p. 4.

[9] Thomas Paine, *The Rights of Man* (Part II), in Harry Hayden Clark (ed.), *op. cit.,* pp. 176, 178.

but managed to survive in order. Most of the time, and in most of its forms, the worst enemy of mankind is government: it is the fountain of almost all the evil and suffering in society.

These arguments are supplemented by later liberal thinkers (whose heirs, men like Friedrich von Hayek and Bertrand de Jouvenel, are still writing today). Though not liberal in most respects, Bentham also made his contribution. These arguments may be sorted as follows:

1. All restriction is painful. But pleasure is the only good. Therefore when government has done the indispensable minimum, it should do no more. Otherwise its restrictions (laws supported by the threat or use of force, by the system of punishment) increase the amount of pain in society. (Bentham.)

2. All restriction is, by definition, a contravention of freedom. But freedom is the highest good. Government exists to protect freedom, but after a certain point, its restrictions in behalf of freedom become encroachments on freedom. Therefore the more limited government is, the better. (Spencer most emphatically, and Mill some of the time.)

3. Men know their own business best and do not need government to help them conduct their affairs. The emphasis here is on economic matters. What they need is security. (Bentham, Spencer, and Mill some of the time.)

4. Government tends to be inefficient, and when it intervenes it meddles and retards efficiency. By retarding efficiency it interferes with men in pursuit of their goals. (Bentham, Spencer, and Mill.)

5. Give government an opening into an area of life, and it will do everything possible to perpetuate its role, even after it is no longer of any use. Governments hunger after power, and their hunger increases with its satisfaction. They have an inevitable encroaching tendency which must not be encouraged. (Spencer and Mill.)

6. The common good is freedom. But freedom is valuable for the growth of individuality. Individuality cannot flourish, energy cannot be elicited, human faculties cannot develop, if government is too constant and too pervasive a presence. (Mill.)

Recommendations Concerning Restrictions on Government

No political theory is free of some explicit or implicit principle which is meant to serve either as an inhibition on the action of government or as a justification for the people (as individuals, in groups, or as a whole) to check (in some way or other) the action of government, or both. These principles can be applied in the real world as well as in the ideal political system recommended by a given political theorist. They are formulated with universal intent. They pertain to the scope of governmental activity as well as to the procedures by which those activities are carried out. Some of the main ones are the following.

a. Prudence. Though Hobbes will not countenance any principle which the people may use to declare governmental action illegitimate, a reading of *Leviathan* makes it clear that Hobbes expects government not only to be the guarantor of peace between men in society, but also to act in such a way as not to incite men to war on it. Certainly Hobbes thought it took very little for men to be bellicose; fear of pain or punishment was vastly more efficacious than men's reason in compelling them to remain at peace. But in Chapter 15, Hobbes lists some of the qualities of human behavior that tend to discourage bellicosity: justice, gratitude, modesty, equity, mercy, and so on. These qualities are enjoined on all men:

> These dictates of reason, men used to call by the name of laws, but improperly: for they are but conclusions, or theorems concerning what conduceth to the conservation and defence of themselves; whereas law, properly, is the word of him, that by right hath command over others. But yet if we consider the same theorems, as delivered in the word of God, that by right commandeth all things; then they are properly called laws.[10]

Though the people cannot hold government accountable when it fails to conform to these "theorems"—the ruler is accountable only to God— it is reasonable to suppose that Hobbes wanted government so to conform, if only out of the sane wish to keep the established order intact. That sane wish is best called prudence, and counsels of prudence figure prominently in many works of political theory. Prudence is instrumental to the common good, however defined; and in one of its most important forms, it is a counsel of forbearance: advice to accept restrictions on what government should do and how government should do it.

b. Rule of Law. The demand for the rule of law is the demand for regularity or certainty, and hence for the avoidance of its contraries, namely, arbitrary, capricious, unpredictable behavior on the part of government. The source of the idea is to be found in Plato and Aristotle. In *The Statesman* (302), Plato distinguishes good forms of government from their respective perversions on the basis of their adherence to the rule of law: good ones do, bad ones do not adhere. (Plato also says that in the ideal political order, presumably the one constructed in *The Republic*, the wisdom of the rulers cancels the necessity for the rule of law, though conceivably the rule of law may exist there.) It is Aristotle, however, who fiercely praises the rule of law, and who is, on that account, reckoned the father of the idea. In the *Politics*, he says:

> And the rule of law, it is argued, is preferable to that of any individual. On the same principle, even if it be better for certain individuals

---

[10] Hobbes, *op. cit.*, pp. 104–105.

to govern, they should be made only guardians and ministers of the law. . . . Therefore he who bids the law rule may be deemed to bid God and Reason alone rule, but he who bids man rule adds an element of the beast; for desire is a wild beast, and passion perverts the minds of rulers, even when they are the best of men. The law is reason unaffected by desire.[11]

The last sentence quoted from Aristotle indicates that for him the rule of law necessarily incorporates the demand for just laws. Locke is even clearer on this point. He says:

Absolute Arbitrary Power, or Governing without settled standing Laws, can neither of them consist with the ends of Society and Government, which Men would not quit the freedom of the state of Nature for, and tie themselves up under, were it not to preserve their Lives, Liberties and Fortunes; and by stated Rules of Right and Property to secure their Peace and Quiet.[12]

But for others, the rule of law is a formal matter, independent of the content of the laws, and best summed up in old adages like no crime without a law, no punishment without a crime; all men are entitled to the equal protection of the laws; no man stands in privilege outside the law. Or for others, the rule of law is a procedural matter, confining government to certain methods in dealing with suspects, accused persons, and criminals. It must act in accordance with due process of law, the main particulars of which are listed in Article I (Section 9) and in amendments 4 through 8 of the American Constitution. Furthermore, owing to the example of American practice of living by a written Constitution, a document containing the *fundamental law* of the political system has been included by some in the rule of law. The underlying principle is that arrangements dealing with the structure and scope of governmental power, and the processes of election, are so crucial that they necessitate as much explicitness as possible. Essential to the concept is that government by itself cannot institute changes in the arrangement. Rather, the component or constituent parts of the nation—however those parts are defined—must consent, and consent usually by more than a bare majority. In any case, worship—that is not too strong a word—of the rule of law is one of the most constant themes in the history of political theory. It is seen as instrumental to the common good, however defined: much in life depends on regularity of expectation. And even at its most formal it embodies a respect for persons, and hence contributes directly to the high moral ends which the various kinds of substantive common good

[11] Aristotle, *Politics* (III, 16), trans. Benjamin Jowett, in Richard McKeon (ed.), *op. cit.*, p. 1202.

[12] Locke, *op. cit.* (XI, 137), p. 377.

also serve. The practices and procedures of a political system are thus sometimes as morally valuable as the net outcome of its workings.

c. Higher Law. Like almost all political ideas, the idea of higher law is Greek in origin. In general, the phrase designates a principle or set of principles, not man-made but deriving from a source greater than man, which should serve as a standard for the activities and policies of government, and which can be used by the people to judge, favorably or adversely, those activities and policies. The will of God, the order of Nature, the purposes of Nature, the conclusions of pure Mind have all figured as touchstones for human or positive laws, and other political matters. The assumption is that because the source of these principles is not human, but transcendental, they have an unimpeachable validity which nothing merely human can begin to approximate. Most cynically put, transcendental sources are able to lend a prestige to political arguments that such arguments could acquire in no other way. The further assumption is that the principles, when realized on earth, will lead to the greatest good of mankind: the transcendental source is purely benevolent.

Plato, Aristotle, the Stoics, the major thinkers in the Christian traditions (both Catholic and Protestant), and secular thinkers in the seventeenth and eighteenth centuries look beyond humanity to discover their definitions of the common good, and to be guided in their detailed practical recommendations. Whether the higher law goes by the name of natural right or natural law or divine revelation, men have a standard to hold up against the way of the world and, most importantly, to find it wanting. In potentiality, the variants of the doctrine of the higher law are instruments of serious censure directed against prevailing political (and social) institutions. It must be said, however, that the *systematic* critical use of higher law is mostly the work of the seventeenth and eighteenth centuries, when higher law is termed natural law. It must also be said that one of the most careful and subtle treatments of natural law, with all the difficulties of ascertaining its content and applying it in particular circumstances, is that of Aquinas. Any thought about the subject must begin with his writing, even though he is infinitely more cautious in his use of the doctrine for critical and reformist purposes than later thinkers.

d. Absolute Rights. There are some claims or entitlements—to use two words roughly synonymous with rights—which, according to various political traditions dating back to the Middle Ages, governments must recognize as restraints in their dealings with the people. The content of natural law, as described by Aquinas, would lead to the assertion that no government may kill or maim an innocent person, or interfere with the integrity of his "normal" sexuality, the choice of his spouse, or the conduct of his family life, or impede him in his search (instructed by the Church, of course) for the truth about God, or do anything that, in general, would disrupt men's social life. On the other hand, medieval notions, most famously summarized in the Magna Charta of 1215, imposed on the king prohibitions dealing with his subjects' properties, freedoms, and immunities. However, it is not until the seventeenth century in England that the doctrine of rights becomes a much bolder and more inclusive theory, and does so by centering on the individual and the guarantees (or "fences," to use Locke's word) required to sustain him as a rational creature. The common good is achieved precisely when government provides those guarantees for the individual—against other individuals, but also and equally important, against the government itself.

In the early parts of the *Second Treatise,* Locke labors to convince the reader that the source of rights is a God-given endowment granted to all men at birth. Even before governments existed, when men lived in a state of nature, all men recognized these rights in each other: they could live in the state of nature only because most men had sufficient rationality and good will to confer such recognition on each other. The function of government is to shore up this mutual recognition. At the same time, it must not become itself the cause of infringement of these rights. Locke in effect claims to have read the mind of God and deduced from his reading the theory of rights. Paine dispenses with reference to pre-governmental conditions: he does not feel the need to support his views with mock-historical conjecture. He comes right out and says, "Natural rights are those which appertain to man in right of his existence." What it means to be human depends strictly on the guarantee of rights: men's claims and entitlements must be honored if men are to be truly human. And as Locke and Hobbes go beyond the inherited tradition to make slavery incompatible with natural rights, Paine goes beyond Locke in making intellectual freedom a natural right: Locke's defense of tolerance, though made on grounds of natural right and other, pragmatic grounds as well, is primarily devoted to religious matters. The First Amendment of the American Constitution flatly asserts these intellectual rights against government, even though it does not provide a rationale for them. (That rationale was to come in the course of numerous decisions of the United States Supreme Court and was to omit Nature and Nature's God as its basis.)

We must also notice that though we have spoken of rights as absolute, some encroachments have proved necessary. For example, the heart of Locke's political theory is solicitude for private property. Yet Locke knew that government, which exists to protect property, could not exist without money collected in the form of taxes. Locke only stipulated that whatever the form of government, there be no taxation without consent. For another example, the United States government has denied free speech to some when speech presents a "clear and present danger" to government and hence to society. Incitement to violence or sedition is thus not protected by the guarantees of the First Amendment.

But despite these qualifications—and the subject is entirely too large and complex for us to do more than mention it—various rights have been defended absolutely by various political theorists, especially since the seventeenth century. It would be safe to say that for us the most familiar species of inhibition on governmental activity is the doctrine of absolute rights. Or given the record of American experience, one should perhaps call it the doctrine of nearly absolute, or *prima facie* absolute, rights. Which is to say that in some cases the absoluteness of certain rights may have to yield to conflicting but more weighty considerations, though the yielding must be marginal, and the case for yielding must be greeted with a strong initial skepticism.

e. **Conscience.** In Chapter 29 of *Leviathan*, Hobbes says that, "another doctrine repugnant to civil society is, that whatsoever a man does against his conscience, is sin; and it dependeth on the presumption of making himself judge of good and evil."[13] Hobbes goes on to belittle the claims of conscience as irrational subjectivism, and sees in them the road to irreconcilable divergences of opinion and hence to tumult and civil war. But despite Hobbes's ire, the claims of conscience have been put forth by Catholic and Protestant writers alike, and by writers not strictly religious as well. The problems of conscience emerge in two situations. In the first, individuals or groups are commanded by government to profess a faith, and to worship in ways, they find unholy. In the second, individuals or groups are commanded by government to act in certain ways that offend their highest principles. In both cases the penalties for disobedience may be severe.

The first situation arises only in societies that do not guarantee freedom of religion. Even the most authoritarian theorists, like Luther, say that the subject is not morally obliged to obey his government when his government offends against true religion. (He speaks for Protestants oppressed by Catholic government. What he says in behalf of Catholic and heretical subjects of Protestant rulers is inconsistent. Luther, like many religious writers, does not have a general theory of conscience.) Luther counsels noncompliance, but rejects active resistance to authority in the name of conscience. Men must disobey and also take the penalties for their disobedience: Luther preaches the doctrine of civil disobedience. Others, like Aquinas and Calvin, permit even active resistance against authority, if conscience is seriously "scandalized."

The second situation may arise in all societies. In modern times, the names of Thoreau, Tolstoy, and Gandhi, all political moralists, come to mind as advocates of conscience against both democratic and nondemo-

---

[13] Hobbes, *op. cit.*, p. 211.

cratic government. If a general view can be distilled from these writers, it would be: (1) the offense against conscience must be grave, so grave as to involve the existence of radical evil over a long period of time; (2) the claims couched in the language of conscience must make reference to moral principles commonly held but not acted on, and not to individual intuition or uncommunicable private experience; (3) the normal processes of politics must seem clogged, and change for the better must appear wholly unlikely anytime in the future. Thoreau, Tolstoy, and Gandhi are all considered apostles of nonviolence, resembling Luther in this regard. But the resemblance is not complete, for two reasons. First, all three men approve policies far less passive than Luther: they encourage movements to disturb government in innumerable ways, and think that government will be budged only if there are such movements. Second, there are passages in Thoreau's "Civil Disobedience" that indicate a readiness to contemplate the use of violence. In any case, it would be safe to say that when the claims of conscience are advanced, either in matters of religion or of broad social policy, the typical moral recommendation is for civil disobedience: the politics of conscience is characteristically a tender politics. The claims of conscience may thus be advanced for the sake of the common good, or for the sake of higher ends to which the common good is deemed instrumental.

Recommendations Concerning Form of Government

In its broadest sense, the phrase "form of government" has been used to refer to three main characteristics of the political process. The first is the number of people involved directly or indirectly in the activities of rule. The second is the social class or classes in whose interest rule is predominantly exercised. The third is (to use Montesquieu's word) the "principle" of the political process: that is, the sentiments or ideals which give the prevailing hue to the motives and goals of those involved directly or indirectly in the activities of rule.[14]

It is instructive to follow Aristotles reasoning on forms or "constitutions" in Books III through VI in the *Politics*. He begins with the number of people involved: one, few, or many: monarchy, aristocracy, polity; and their respective "perversions": tyranny, oligarchy, and democracy. He then indicates that to speak only of number does not suffice for the purposes of analysis.

> The argument seems to show that, whether in oligarchies or in democracies, the number of the governing body, whether the greater number, as in a democracy, or the smaller number, as in an oligarchy, is an accident due to the fact that the rich are everywhere few, and

---

[14] Baron de Montesquieu, *The Spirit of the Laws* (III, 1), trans. Thomas Nugent (New York: Hafner, 1949), p. 19.

the poor numerous. But if so, there is a misapprehension of the causes of the difference between them. For the real difference between democracy and oligarchy is poverty and wealth.[15]

After thus correcting the conventional mode of classifying constitutions, Aristotle goes on to determine the spirit that gives life to them. Oligarchies, for example, are dominated by a total solicitude for the acquisition and security of wealth; and all political arrangements and social policies, as well as general beliefs and habits, look to wealth first and last. On the other hand, "The basis of a democratic state is liberty. . . . One principle of liberty is for all to rule and be ruled in turn . . . whence it follows that the majority must be supreme . . . Another is that a man should live as he likes."[16] Aristotle also stresses the fact that each form has many varieties. The "principle" and the bias of class interest remain constant in all the varieties, but the number of people involved in rule (the size of the body of citizens) may vary, as may other traits, like the kind of socioeconomic classes that make up society, the procedures for choosing rulers, and the relations of parts of government to each other.

The subject of "forms of government" is therefore considerably more complicated than the words themselves seem to suggest. When studied in accordance with Aristotle's scheme, as it has been by Montesquieu and many of the most famous political theorists, political scientists, and sociologists since Hegel's time, it is no mere recital of mechanical devices and procedures. It deals with more than the formal institutions of power. When measured by Aristotle's scheme, and by his own execution of it, the literature of political theory leaves itself open to two judgments. First, in considering forms, some political theorists content themselves with mechanical and institutional recommendations. They do not go on, as Aristotle did, to consider the social and psychological bases of their recommendations. Locke, for example, is too mechanical in his approach. Second, the subject of forms, perhaps more than any other taken up by political theorists, requires the student to go outside the works of political theory to the works of political science, general or specific, for deeper understanding. It is instructive to recall that Aristotle wrote a detailed study, *Constitution of Athens*, which "formed part of an extensive collection of histories of the constitutions of one hundred and fifty-eight cities and tribes, most of them Greek."[17] The forms recommended by political theorists are patterned on existing forms, and one's judgment of the recommended forms must depend on as extensive a knowledge as possible of the forms as they are embodied, and as they operate, in the real world. For a long time, the names of forms of government were borrowed

[15] Aristotle, *Politics* (III, 8), in Richard McKeon (ed.), *op. cit.*, pp. 1186–87.
[16] *Ibid.* (III, 9), pp. 1187–89; (VI, 2), pp. 1265–66.
[17] Kurt von Fritz and Ernst Kapp, "Introduction," *Aristotle's Constitution of Athens and Related Texts*, (New York: Hafner, 1950), p. 3.

from Aristotle: monarchy, aristocracy, the mixed state, oligarchy, democracy, and tyranny. At times, the rule of priests or theocracy was included. Recently, the categories of representative government, dictatorship, party dictatorship, authoritarian government, and totalitarian dictatorship have had currency, in response to the emergence of apparently new forms of government. We cannot enter here into all the desirable distinctions and refinements. Rather we must be satisfied with a simplification, which is this: when we survey all the forms recommended in the literature of political theory, whatever their name, we will find that they fall into three categories. Two of the categories are suggested by C. P. Snow in his *Science and Government*: "closed politics" and "open politics." "Closed politics" is "any kind of politics in which there is no appeal to a larger assembly."[18] "Open politics" is any kind in which there is such appeal at least on the major decisions. We add the third or "mixed" category, which combines open and closed elements. In most cases, the recommended form has an important relation to the given definition of the common good. The relation is either one of strong preference by the theorist, or one of instrumental (practical) *necessity,* or one of *both* instrumental and moral necessity. In a few cases, the common good is so defined as to include a specific form in the very definition. And in a few cases, little is made of the whole matter of forms: as long as government has appropriate powers and scope, and recognizes the appropriate principle (or principles) of restriction, government may take any form consonant with circumstances.

Those few who make little of the matter of forms are guided by the feeling best expressed in Epistle III of Pope's *An Essay on Man*:

> For Forms of Government let fools contest;
> Whate'er is best administered is best.

In much of his writing, Bentham seems willing to accept any existent form provided those who rule seek to extend the happiness and lessen the suffering of their subjects as much as possible. Spencer and some of his disciples write in a setting of open politics in the form of representative government which they take for granted. But they indicate there is no practical or moral necessity for it: it is conceivable that liberty—but most crucially, liberty of contract (free use of one's property)—could be preserved in nonrepresentative forms of government. Indeed, the gravest threat to liberty of contract could very well come from representative government when suffrage is extended to most or all in society. The poor would use political power to redistribute wealth.

We need not dwell on those few—Plato, Aristotle, Machiavelli, Rousseau, and Hegel—whose definition of the common good is a pattern

---

[18] C. P. Snow, *Science and Government* (New York: Mentor, 1962), p. 53.

or process of politics. We have already paid some attention to their arguments in Chapter II. Plato's rule of the wise is a renowned (and usually deplored) instance of closed politics. Aristotle and Rousseau present versions of open politics, though in Aristotle's case, it must be remembered that many inhabitants—serfs and slaves—are excluded from citizenship. Machiavelli and Hegel present versions of mixed politics, in which the hereditary element (nobility for Machiavelli; ample kingly powers and nobility for Hegel) and the element of merit (a powerful bureaucracy for Hegel), coexist with the popular element (direct participation for Machiavelli; representation and consultation for Hegel).

It is those cases in which some necessity is claimed for a specific form, or some strong preference voiced, that deserve our closer, though brief, scrutiny.

Speaking very roughly, we can say that when closed politics is recommended, whether in the form of monarchic government or a council of rulers, where the ultimate power of making and enforcing laws is entrusted to one man or a few men, efficiency is the ground either for a strong preference or for the assertion of instrumental necessity. It is thought that peace, the great end desired by the Augustinian tradition and by Hobbes, requires simplicity in the procedure of decision-making and unity in the overall direction of affairs. To grant the people or their representatives any share in politics is to invite confusion and dissension, and thus to imperil peace. To be sure, Hobbes holds out the theoretical possibility of open politics: all the people gathered in a sovereign assembly may wield the powers of the leviathan. But it is clear that Hobbes has no taste for such a prospect; he is certain that under such conditions politics will degenerate into riot. Within the range of closed politics (king or council), Hobbes's strong preference is for kingly government. Let it be noted that those who advocate kingly government know perfectly well that the activities of rule require the labors of more than one man: there must be advisers and assistants. The point is that the great decisions and the ultimate responsibility are the monarch's, and against his word there can be, in principle, no dissent and no recourse. We should also notice that the Augustinian tradition, and the tradition of divine-right absolute monarchy supply subsidiary arguments to shore up the institution of the monarchy. God's will, or God's gift, or the model of one God as ruler of the universe plays a part in the rhetoric of these versions of closed politics. But the central consideration is efficiency in the name of peace.

The great theorist of mixed politics is Aristotle. What he says on this subject is merely amplified (and not always for the better), or variously applied, by later theorists, even those who did not know his work at first-hand. It is, however, not in his capacity as advocate of the ideal system of politics that he writes on mixed politics, but rather as one who tries to teach the world how to attain a system that, though not ideal, is reasonably decent, and certainly better than the common forms of democracy and oligarchy. The essence of his position is that in a society made up of several social classes, and hence of inequalities of wealth and status, justice (the preservation of every man in his own) can be assured only if each class has enough power to protect itself and not enough to encroach on the position of others. Aristotle suggests a number of ways by which this distribution of power can be institutionally realized, and we need not enter into the details. The important idea is that class warfare, which inevitably is resolved by one species of injustice or another, can be avoided only if total class rule is avoided. Aristotelian mixed politics is a compromise between the elements of numbers and wealth. It is thus instrumentally necessary for justice (the common good) in all but the ideal constitution. Among others, Polybius, Cicero, Aquinas, Montesquieu, Burke, and Madison (when allowance is made for the peculiarities of American experience), all follow Aristotle's lead. All are, it should be mentioned, concerned with the preservation of a just order, and are driven to Aristotle's solution. Clearly, the preservation of a just order is, at the same time, the preservation of inequalities: the idea of using political power to ameliorate the condition of the poor at the expense of the rich is ruled out as inherently unjust. Mixed politics rests on the forbearance of the rich and the passivity of the poor. It is no accident that Aristotle thought the existence of a sizable middle class as a balancer of power the precondition of mixed politics. It takes a situation of phenomenal growth in the means of production to accustom men—although some resist, and with a tenacious rancor—to the very notion that poverty can be ameliorated on a large scale, and in a decisive way. We should also observe that a mechanical species of mixed politics is found in Locke's political theory; the hallowed doctrine of the separation of the (preferably elected) legislative power from the (hereditary) executive power is enunciated by him. But the class basis is missing from Locke's account. His fear is mainly of executive arrogance, of the tendency of power to corrupt the holder of it, and he thinks he sees in the separation of powers a method of immunization against corruption.

Open politics is quite simply the politics of numbers. Its tenet is that all men (or citizens or adults) are entitled to take part (personally or through their representatives) in making the ultimate decisions that affect their lives. In representative systems, all men should be granted the vote, there are periodic elections, all votes should weigh equally, the majority determines the election, the representatives vote in accordance with the sense of their constituency, majority rule obtains among the representatives, and there are no restrictions on the will of the majority of the representatives except for common morality, or the higher law, or absolute rights, or the fundamental law.

The suppositions are that elections are necessary if those in power are to know the wishes of the electorate; the electorate can be counted on to know best what it wishes; the electorate can be counted on, by and large, to be morally trustworthy and intellectually competent; men in power must be faced by the prospect of the periodic scrutiny of elections if they are not to grow slack or insensitive or irresponsible in office. When the common good is defined as either freedom or the facilitation of social change, a strong case can be made to show that open politics is instrumentally necessary. The case fails of absolute conclusiveness only because—as Mill and most theorists of open politics know—a certain degree of wealth and civilization may first have to be attained before open politics works as it is supposed to work. The fate of open politics in "backward" countries bears witness only too sadly to the fact that open politics must have roots if it is to endure.

What is so interesting about open politics is that its broad features can also be advocated on grounds of moral necessity (as well as those of instrumental necessity). The instrumental necessities do not exhaust the reasons for recommending it. In the theory of open politics, whether direct or representative, there are two reasons that have been given for its moral necessity. The first reason is active. Taking part in politics, even in a small way, liberates human energies, intensifies the duty of rational behavior, and bestows a sense of dignity and self-worth as no other kind of politics can. (In modern times, Paine, Mill, and Dewey have reasoned in this manner.) Thus, open politics is characterized as essentially educative. Its processes not only guarantee freedom and the facilitation of social change, but they contribute directly to the growth of moral personality, the finest manifestations of which do not have to be political at all. The second reason is passive. The prime features of open politics, like universal suffrage (political equality) and majority rule, are in themselves illustrations of that respect for persons which is the source of defining the common good as freedom or the facilitation of social change. The processes of open politics not only result in the most that can be politically achieved for persons; they also help make society a society of persons by treating them according to the demands of equality and responsivenes. (As we have seen, similar notions have been applied to due process of law.) The late Sir Ernest Barker went so far as to say that

> the way of democracy . . . is not a solution, but a way of seeking solutions . . . The core of democracy is choice, and not something chosen.[19]

---

[19] Ernest Barker, *Principles of Social and Political Theory* (Oxford: Clarendon Press, 1951), p. 207.

At a time when many defenders of open politics, alarmed at public apathy and irrationality, executive aggrandizement, and the often free play of narrow interests, confine their *apologia* to the practical necessities, it is good to recall that other lines of defense exist and serve as an inspiration for reform.

Chapter IV

THE USES OF
POLITICAL THEORY

It is no secret that the study of "the old books" of political theory has fallen on hard times. Those who teach the subject in America feel like an unwanted minority, not so much persecuted as ignored, or when not ignored, brushed aside as obscure or irrelevant. According to a recent study of the profession of political science in the United States, political theory ranked last among seven fields of political study "in the esteem of the profession." Political scientists were asked "to identify . . . the field(s) of political science in which they felt that the *most* and the *least* significant work was being done."[1] The ratio of "favorable to unfavorable mentions" was lowest for political theory. Even those respondents who were themselves teachers of political theory could muster only enough enthusiasm to place political theory fourth. In the face of such skepticism it is necessary (though perhaps quixotic) to try to make some statement about the use of political theory as contained in the old books.

There are many reasons for reading the works of political theory. They will fascinate anyone concerned with the history of ideas and concepts, or with the history of moral consciousness, or with the history of responses to political crises, or with the integrity or internal consistency

[1] Albert Somit and Joseph Tanenhaus, *American Political Science: A Profile of a Discipline* (New York: Atherton, 1964), pp. 55–56.

of bodies of abstract thought, or with the spectacle of superior minds endeavoring to master an area of inquiry, the intricate vastness of which must finally evade the grasp of even superior minds. But despite that, one still wants to feel that the study of political theory can also, in fact, promote the study of politics, can play a part in the enrichment of political science. How then can it do so?

Before the question, Of what use are the old books of political theory? can be taken up, a prior question must be asked. That question is, What do we expect of the political scientist? The worth of political theory, from the point of view of the political scientist, depends on the tasks he sets himself. At the risk of pretentiousness, at the risk of seeming to legislate for an entire profession, let us explore briefly the question of tasks.

What Is Asked of a Political Scientist: In Everyday Life

When ordinary or sophisticated people turn to the political scientist as an expert, they are looking for several things. The subject can be politics in the usual sense, or politics in a sense extended to include all sorts of organizations, committees, informal associations, and relations involving the exertion of influence and the competition of wills and aims. The range is from nations to clubs. What people want first is *advice*. They want advice on structural matters, on how to revise or arrange the formal relation of offices to each other, on how to distribute authority and allocate responsibilities. Or they want advice on policies. What is to be done in a given crisis or predicament, or in a threatened one, or in case a new opportunity presents itself? What is needed to maintain or restore soundness? What can be done to improve a general condition? How can the inevitable periods of transition be best handled? Or they want advice on tactics, on the execution of plots, on the employment of cunning, on the exploitation of human frailty, on attaining, securing, and increasing control.

What they want second is that the political scientist engage in acts of *inference*. If the first kind of advice is largely though not exclusively sought by those at the top, this second kind of advice is largely though not exclusively sought by those underneath. The normal status of those underneath is to be, and to be kept, at least partly in the dark about what is going on, about the way in which things are developing, about the difference between appearances and reality, between what is said and what is meant, and between what is said and what is intended. Governors love secrets, and sometimes need to keep the secrets they so love to have. Then too, if as Norman Mailer says, there is "magic" at the top, there is also confusion, self-ignorance, disarray, and division. These characteristics join with secrecy to make the activities of leaders and policy-makers often dismally obscure. Standing on the outside, the curious and the worried look to the political scientist to enlarge their political understanding. He is expected to make the effort of piecing things together, of attributing motives, of bringing to bear on a particular situation an acquaintance with analogous situations in the past.

What they want third is skill in *speculation* about the near future, a skill closely related to the capacity for inference. Again relying on his knowledge of completed patterns in the past, the political scientist is called on to ponder the tendencies in the present and to project them further, to display some competence in the art of conjecture. Political journalists are professionally addicted to this enterprise, and though we mock them we read them compulsively and rely on them quite heavily. Nothing so ambitious as prediction or prophecy is sought, despite the lack of humility and tentativeness frequently characterizing speculation. The proper intention is the pursuit of possibilities, a glimpse of vague movements, a detection of the sources of novelty and eruption.

In short, the common expectation is that the political scientist is absorbed by his interest in the present and the near future; and that because of his acquaintance with the political past (importantly similar to the present) and with political devices, and because of his proclivity for scrutinizing motives and for being suspicious, perhaps dirty-minded, he can give advice, infer an approximation to the truth, and speculate plausibly. It would probably be safe to say that most political scientists would not find it insulting to be guided by the common expectation in defining one aspect of their calling. Some everyday, practical insight is surely not a meager indication of professional application to the study of politics.

What Political Scientists Ask of Themselves: To Philosophize about Practice

But what more is expected? What should political scientists expect of themselves? At this point, as we know, divergent opinions press their claims. What is the nature of the professional contribution a political scientist ought to make to political science? How is it to be described in an overall way, apart from the division of political science into numerous fields?

On the basis of a measure of familiarity with American political science of the past generation, one could say that some in the profession (and of those, some of the most distinguished) have insisted that the political scientist is, ideally, philosophical (or theoretical), whatever else he may choose to be. By "philosophical" is here meant not an adherence to a metaphysical system, but a willingness to engage in all those intellectual enterprises dealing with political practice we mentioned in Chapter III. American political science has really wrestled with a great number of issues that arise when the political spectator moves back a little from his everyday absorption in politics, and tries to be more careful, more self-conscious, less bewitched by particularity, less caught up in the needs or delights of the moment. This intellectual distance is the precondition for philosophizing about political practice. It cannot be denied that American political scientists have sought that distance precisely to be able to think about politics philosophically. Indeed, though it may sound ungrateful to say so, the seeking for distance has appeared at times to be too single-minded, with the result that political studies suffer from aridity and abstractness, show no esthetic pleasure taken in the seductive surface of politics, and betray some lack of involvement in matters which it may be almost impious to discuss coolly and philosophically. It is a fact that philosophizing about the moral life and making recommendations concerning ends and means seldom accompany current philosophizing about practice. But most would agree that despite the risk of making politics uninteresting, those who are willing to take up the burden of philosophy should be encouraged in their endeavor. Though the results are inconclusive, even contradictory, we all benefit. We need the play of many "searchlights," as Karl Popper puts it, on the wild field of politics.

What Political Scientists Ask of Themselves: To Be Scientific

It would be foolish to think, however, that the bulk of American political science has been addressed to the philosophical aspects of the study of politics. Some larger mission has occupied the center of concerns, and that of course has been to commence the creation of the science of politics. For many, the question of whether the study of politics can be a science is a closed question. Not only can it be practiced as a science, but if it is not, it will be only triviality or daydreaming, an incredible squandering of intellectual resources. The heart of the political scientist's claim to be professional lies in his ability to be a scientist.

What then does it mean to be scientific? From the literature of American political science, three answers emerge. The first is that to be scientific means to have a certain kind of temperament: to be free of passion and prejudice when one is studying some political subject or other. It is thought that only the attitude of the outside (but knowledge-able) observer is suitable for anyone who seeks to speak the truth about politics. Politics itself is soaked in the passions and prejudices of its contestants: to be partisan, partial, self-interested, hypocritical, indifferent to the merits of the case, oblivious to the claims or interests of others, is to be political. If the political scientist shares in these qualities, the cause of truth or accuracy is sacrificed. The pity is that the study of politics, perhaps more than any other study, is likely to arouse these very qualities. The morality of the political scientist, which is the morality of truth, depends on the elimination of such traits to the fullest degree possible. The inordinately difficult act of self-transcendence is indispensable if the political scientist is to be faithful to his calling.

The second answer is that to be scientific is to assert nothing that has not been verified, and to propose no hypothesis that cannot, in principle, be verified. Mere hunch or guesswork or stale repetition of received opinion simply does not qualify as verified or verifiable statement. In turn, verification entails direct observation of the condition being described. And that, in turn, is sometimes thought to entail the translation of perceived truths into the language of mathematics, so that all ambivalence and inexactitude are shunned.

The third answer is that to be scientific is to aspire toward the creation of a continuously growing body of political knowledge, each addition to which derives from the extant body of political knowledge and is verified empirically, a body of knowedge which one day can attain a reasonable completeness. The body of knowledge grows as hypotheses derived from it are seen to be verified and as their number increases. The premise is that the study of politics is the study of invariant regularities, invariant relationships. In a given situation, men will act in one and only one way. The necessary and sufficient conditions for any species of political behavior, for any political act, gesture, decision, tendency, can be specified. The foundation of political science, thus construed, is the science of human behavior. Politics is the congeries of regular and predictable emanations of human nature. Psychological determinism is the necessary article of belief, while other sorts of determinism which involve, in T. S. Eliot's phrase, "vast, impersonal forces," are now ignored or held to be discredited. To be sure, the interest of the political scientist is not in the entire realm of psychological knowledge, but is rather centered on that portion of the realm which deals with traits of character that normally figure in politics—traits like fear, anger, pride, envy, competitiveness, guilt, honor, spite, desire for gain, and desire for sheer survival in a tolerable status. It must be added, however, that no psychological datum can be ruled out *a priori*; some finding once thought beside the point can, as political knowledge deepens, suddenly acquire relevance. It is just that the political scientist will place greater emphasis on, and make greater use of, some portions of the realm of psychological knowledge than others.

Now if the roles of the political scientist as everyday expert and as philosopher go unchallenged, his role as literally a political scientist has met with a good amount of opposition, from within the profession of political science as well as from within the profession of philosophy and such related professions as history. I believe that much of that opposition is well founded. These matters are naturally too massive to be treated with any adequacy in a short space. But I do think a little should be said, because the question of the use of the old books of political theory is decisively affected by the view that political science must be practiced as a science very much like the natural sciences. In fact, each of the three preceding interpretations of what it means to be scientific, if pressed to the limit and accepted as primary, would leave very little in the old books deserving of the attention of the political scientist. Moreover, the third interpretation really puts every other conceivable task of the political scientist in the shade. Even if it could be shown, as I think it could, that the old books have much to teach the political scientist in his role as everyday expert and as philosopher, that would be rather paltry in comparison with its ability to teach him anything, or anything but a tiny bit, in his role as scientist, as one who adds his share to a potentially complete system of political knowledge. Surely science is immeasurably greater than ordinary conversation about science; surely philosophy is idle unless it facilitates science.

Let us look at the first interpretation, science as neutrality of temperament. The assertion that politics, more than any other subject, elicits the passions of the student is plausible. That the passions, and the other related human infirmities, can darken the understanding and lead to the dissemination or perpetuation of error is also plausible. But need political scientists rush to the opposite extreme and study politics as a natural scientist studies inert matter, or sentient but unrational creatures? Must political scientists strip themselves of all feeling, all moral engagement, all vicarious participation, when they study politics? I think that answer must be an unequivocal no. There is a third possibility, besides ruthless partisanship and aseptic neutrality. That possibility is defined as a strenuous but volatile combination of detachment and involvement. Without some detachment, perception is killed. The detachment, however, must be compatible with, and is best manifested as, fair-mindedness toward all the contestants whose activities the political scientist examines, and compassion or sympathy for all of them. Without some trace of fairness and compassion, the descriptions of the political scientist will not only be lifeless, but also close to unintelligible. Descriptions of political activities cannot be unfeeling if they are to be verbally adequate to the gravity of the activities themselves. I do not mean to commit the so-called "mimetic fallacy," and hold that a narrative must have the qualities of that which is narrated. I only mean to say that there are tones of voice fit for each kind of intellectual operation. Otherwise that operation is carried out in a highly artificial way that can only mislead the reader. Doubtless now and then a studied neutrality, like that of, say, Hobbes, is powerful and instructive, but it is powerful and instructive exactly because it is exceptional. It is shocking because it is unexpected, and deliberately and wholly out of keeping with the enormity Hobbes was desirous of exposing. He was, that is, a satirist. The neutrality of the political scientist is thus not a pale remoteness, but an ample generosity extended to all but the worst "villains" (to use Machiavelli's word for those few utterly out-side the pale of historical sympathy).

The involvement, on the other hand, injects the needed element of intensity. Coherent descriptions of political activities proceed partly by way of reenactment. Unless the political scientist makes the effort of placing himself in the position of those whose deeds he is recording, he will not comprehend those deeds. He will understand others with the required depth of understanding only if he brings his own self-knowledge to bear. He insensibly becomes part of what he tells. His prime method of verification is by reference to his own feelings and impulses and calculations. How then can he hold himself aloof, and still perform his task? Even more, he must bring some moral commitment to his studies.

One can distinguish between moral commitment and reckless par-tisanship. Moral commitment (when chastened by fairness and compas-sion) is the source of two mandatory features of political writing. First, it is the source of vitality, and vitality is the source of rhetorical strength, and hence of the capacity to educate and enlighten. Scrupulous scholar-ship by itself cannot serve as an instrument of communication. The great and the good works of political writing are rarely boring: they are read and remembered, they teach and provoke, because they are readable. They could not be readable without the disciplined presence of the moral personality of the author. Second, moral commitment is the source of perception. To see in any but a casual or superficial way depends on a developed but refined sense of right and wrong. Of course different political scientists will judge moral matters differently; their moral per-spectives are not uniform. That in itself is desirable, for the simple reason that political knowledge often advances through contrariety. But for the contrariety to be genuine, each study of the same subject must derive from some moral commitment. One can add that the moral interest in politics is usually the first and strongest force attracting the mind to political studies, and a sustained absorption in them is continually fed by it.

The second interpretation, science as the verification of hypotheses, must now be considered. In regard to *verification*, who can deny that impatence with self-indulgent, slovenly, or tendentious scholarship is always commendable? But once again, there is some third possibility, besides willful or unself-conscious error and scientific precision. It has often been remarked that only the trivially true in the political and social studies can be demonstrated with absolute finality, and that if absolute finality is demanded, only the trivial will be scrutinized. To avoid triv-iality is imperative. At the same time, the kinds of error into which students of politics are easily led must be avoided. The third possibility is defined by the readiness to remain content with as much certainty as the complexity and elusiveness of politics permit. The mere fact that statements about politics often include reference to motives should indicate that no absolute verification could be possible: secrets, the absence of records, forgetfulness, confusion, the disagreement over intentions between men who cooperate in the same action, the place of unconscious and semiconscious motives, all make the necessary process of scholarly ascription of motives and intentions treacherous in the extreme. No general theory of motivation is fine or subtle enough to make up for unknown particulars. Furthermore, it is notorious that the description of political deeds and policies is inherently ambiguous: the language of political narrative is loaded, and inevitably so, with words open to several constructions. It cannot be cleansed without becoming, most of the time, senseless. And the descriptions made depend on the perspective of the observer: reality alters with the eye of the beholder. One does not mean to dissolve political studies into an all too comfortable and consoling relativism. It is, however, exceedingly unlikely for political scientists to arrive at descriptions or analyses that do not compel, albeit reluctantly, some skepticism. This is the natural condition of political studies, and those in search of scientific precision had better expend their labors in the sciences.

As for the quest for *hypotheses*, it seems to me that this approach to politics is altogether too constricting. Hypotheses are normally expressible in one or two sentences conveying an "if and only if/then" relation of a general sort. Once verified, a hypothesis becomes a proposition, a generality. The place of generalities in political studies is an important one, and we shall shortly come to it. The contention to be made here is that political science is a subject in which the argument, the demonstration, the explanation, the accumulation of narrative ingredients are all as informative and valuable as the conclusion. One can offer a hypothesis, for example, about the origins of the French Revolution of 1789, or the decline of Imperial Spain, or the radical turn of the Supreme Court under Earl Warren. But is it not correct to say that the reader, the student of politics, layman or professional, learns much of what he retains and later uses as the narrative goes on? It is rare that a piece of political explanation is like a puzzle or a riddle, in which the whole point is in the answer or solution. A political narrative or analysis must be seen to be getting somewhere. It must have form; it must have a beginning, a middle, and an end. Ideally, it will leave a residue of instruction behind it. It should not consist of one discrete item followed by another. It should tell a story. Let us notice, for all that, that we do not read stories just to discover how they come out. A writer is judged by all that has gone into his work of explanation, and much of the time he cannot know in advance what parts of his work will be found the most rewarding. More than a series of generalities, political science is an indefinitely large collection of explanations and analyses. One's own store of political science is made up of mastery of such explanations and analyses. Let not *too* much be made, therefore, of the quest for hypotheses.

Last, we must turn to the interpretation of science as a growing body of political knowledge which will one day attain completeness (or near completeness). Political knowledge is viewed as the possession of some number, perhaps very large, of verified propositions capable of explaining all political events and relations, and possibly also of predicting the political future. As we have already said, these propositions or generalities or laws will fully account for political events and relations by specifying the necessary and sufficient conditions for their occurrence. The underlying assumption is that if human nature is thoroughly knowable, so must politics be, for what is politics but human nature in action? In recent years, several philosophers have tried to show that the hope for a science of man or politics or society or historical development is vain. The discontinuity between human behavior and all other natural processes has been stressed; the inadequacy or irrelevance of causal explanations in human matters dwelt on; the distinction between reasons and causes made much of; the logical impossibility of predicting intellectual, esthetic, technological, and hence political and social novelty shown; the place of rules and conventions, the overwhelming significance of language in human life placed in the forefront; the absurdity of mechanistic materialism exposed. The names of H. L. A. Hart,[2] Isaiah Berlin,[3] W. H. Dray,[4] Peter Winch,[5] Michael Scriven,[6] and R. S. Peters,[7] to mention a few, have figured in these fertile but still unterminated discussions which are pervaded by the influence of Wittgenstein and Collingwood. The common theme is that a science of human behavior is, in principle, impossible. It is not a question of insufficient information which more research will remedy. It is rather that much of the time and in many of the most crucial cases, explanation of human behavior cannot be made by reference to truths about human nature, but only by reference to established patterns and conventions of practice which vary from culture to culture, from period to period. There are no invariant relationships. In addition, human behavior cannot normally be understood from the

[2] H. L. H. Hart and A. M. Honoré, *Causation in the Law* (Oxford: Clarendon Press, 1959), Part I.

[3] Isaiah Berlin, "The Concept of Scientific History," in William H. Dray (ed.), *Philosophical Analysis and History* (New York: Harper and Row, 1966), pp. 5–53.

[4] William Dray, *Laws and Explanation in History* (Oxford: Oxford University Press, 1957).

[5] Peter Winch, *The Idea of a Social Science* (London: Routledge and Kegan Paul, 1958).

[6] Michael Scriven, "A Study of Radical Behaviorism," in Herbert Feigl and Michael Scriven (eds.), *The Foundations of Science and the Concepts of Psychology and Psychoanalysis* (Minnesota Studies in the Philosophy of Science, Vol. I.) (Minneapolis: University of Minnesota Press, 1956), pp. 88–130.

[7] R. S. Peters, *The Concept of Motivation* (London: Routledge and Kegan Paul, 1958).

outside, as the habits of animals or the motion of bodies can, but primarily from the inside. A spectator's knowledge does not suffice; it must be supplemented, sometimes replaced, by a participant's knowledge.

For our purposes, the major implications of such reasoning are as follows. First, the body of political knowledge can never attain anything resembling completeness. Political reality does not cease changing; and as it changes, methods of study once appropriate for older kinds of political reality become obsolete, to a great extent if not totally. Reality outstrips the understanding of it, and the best that can be expected is that the understanding will catch up belatedly, and then experience superannuation. Political concepts change with, and in response to, political change. No method of political knowledge can be eternally appropriate; no scientific prediction is thinkable.

Second, the notion of universal and invariant relationships, founded on a science of human behavior, must yield to a notion much less rigorous. The successor notion is one of *systemic* and time-bound relationships which are proposed as likely, not definite or necessary, and which are concerned not with particular individuals and particular acts but with roles and types of action. Political systems must be studied from inside by those fully at home in the culture—those who are alert to the meaning of human activity in the system and are intimately acquainted with the usages, rules, and conventions of the system. No pretense should be made that a systemic generality is other than a tentative statement which usefully describes a connection, but which may be falsified as time goes on, or as new evidence is disclosed. The search for necessary and sufficient conditions must be given up as intolerably inadequate to both the complexities and conventional characteristics of human activity. The folly of predicting countless individual human acts must be renounced.

Third, the only generalities that seem to go beyond the confines of a specific system in a specific period are the generalities of commonplace wisdom. These do derive from an understanding of human nature, but it is the understanding of the great moralists, not that of the scientists of human behavior. There seem to be traits of human nature that have permanent existence, irrespective of time and place, as there are predicaments and situations and patterns of relation that seem continuously to recur throughout history. But two things are clear. First, the proverbs or maxims, numerous as they are, often contradict one another. They are typically epitomes of the moods of passionate and perceptive men trying to get a "handle" on reality. Naturally, exaggeration and disagreement will mark them. Nevertheless, a most worthwhile task of the political scientist is to contribute to the validation of these proverbs and maxims. As for example: power tends to corrupt, political appetites increase with their satisfaction, prestige is the principal motive of political men, the means determine the ends, the means sometimes defeat the ends, the means may become ends in themselves, one thing leads to another, every victory contains the seeds of future trouble, the imperfect is inherently unstable and is defined by excess, and the forms of the imperfect constantly repeat themselves. Politics is truly as rich a field as any for the illustration of common moral phenomena. To search the field for illustrations is to enrich our comprehension of the human condition.

Fourth, allowance should be made for the fact that now and then some conceptual advance is after all made in the study of politics. By "conceptual advance" I mean the emergence of a system of thought which manages, thanks to the thrust of genius, to alter the way in which men thereafter look at the world, past and present. The test is not completeness or exactitude, but suggestiveness. These moments of advance are rare in the history of thought. There is no steady improvement in general political understanding, even though a *specific* political system may be better known after years of constant examination. It would be a rash man who thought that we understood the Greek world of politics better than Thucydides, Plato, and Aristotle, or that we understood our own better than they understood theirs. But occasionally a miracle takes place, the result of which is to let men feel that they now know something no one before them knew. The Marxist and Freudian systems are modern examples.

Let us summarize what we have said so far. The legitimate tasks of the political scientist are to be prepared with advice, inference, and speculation about politics and relations that are political in the extended sense of the term; to engage in a number of intellectual pursuits that can be designated as philosophical, in regard to the study of politics; to avoid taking the mandate of science literally, and instead to abate the demand for verification, to welcome detailed explanations of past and present political phenomena for the sake of political knowledge and not merely for the sake of supporting hypotheses, and to provide such explanations; to know what kinds of generality are possible in political studies and what kinds are not. And I have tried to emphasize the need for moral commitment on the part of the political scientist.

The Uses of Political Theory for the Political Scientist

We must now try to indicate the use of the old books of political theory for the political scientist who accepts the tasks just listed. The first thing to say is that any reader of political theory, any potential user of political theory, must entertain the possibility that the advocacy of political ends, and of their suitable governmental means, can be a serious performance of the mind. Let us remember that the moral voice is the true voice of political theory. There must be no hesitation in saying this, despite the embarrassment or hostility with which the moral voice is heard by some professional political scientists. A political theory is not a flat statement of political (and moral) preference, but an elaborate and wide-ranging defense of a political (and moral) position, with a wide exposure of the writer's mind offered to public criticism, as he seeks to persuade others of his views. Political theory cannot be approached with the conviction that moral discourse is the expression of unsupported feelings, or a sly attempt at manipulative propaganda. That radical disagreement is intrinsic to political theory is not a sign of arbitrary assertion, but rather of the ineffaceably problematic nature of political discussion, whether that discussion is about the facts of an event or situation or about right and wrong, good and bad, the ideal and the imperfect. The sources of moral disagreement are many, including beliefs about God and nature, the good life, the perfection of human character, the availability of resources, and so on—issues that do not permit of proof or definite validation. Just as the tyranny of the scientific model can engender wrong expectations about political science, so it can lead to an impatient disparagement of moral discussion about politics. And just as conclusions on what is the case must normally be met by some skepticism, so moral argument about what is good must forever remain open to contention.

The other possibility that any reader of political theory must entertain is that the desire to preach, to offer to the world a moral critique of the world's political practice, can be a powerful stimulus to perception about politics. We have already said that even in descriptions and explanations of political events and situations (past and present), moral commitment opens the eyes and enlivens the pen as nothing else can. The same consideration holds for those whose aim is not descriptions and explanations of events and situations, but the projection of a political theory. Their starting point is moral commitment; their destination is a vision of the right political system. On the way they will see things, and connections between things, that escape the notice of the uncommitted, if for no other reason, than because the moral critic is constantly on the lookout for faults, in order to justify him in his moral stance. And faults there always are, not commonly exposed and traced to their roots. For imagining something better than reality, critics can see reality better.

The question, therefore, Of what use are the old books of political theory? is nearly self-answering, once the tasks of the political scientist are accepted as they have been given in this chapter and once the qualities of political theory are seen for what they are. Let there be no pretense that the history of the political theory is the history of masterpieces all on the highest level, and all possessed of equal relevance for every generation of men. It is only too obvious that some political theories are more fruitful than others, that some are better executed than others, that most of them have passages of terrible *longueur*, that some contain speculation that will presumably never again excite admiration. Let us also not pretend that the history of political theory is the only source of political insight and method for the political scientist. There are no substitutes for the other sources: political journalism; political history; the accumulated, detailed work of political scientists; works of political science which are cognate to political theory—general, philosophical, or inclusive, but not moral in purpose; the related social sciences; and last, and as important as any, *belles lettres*. Each does what the others cannot do; each is part of the training of the ideal political scientist.

The Uses of Recommendations

To repeat, a political theory is a moral set of inclusive recommendations of a general sort, concerning ends and means, and produced in the course of philosophizing about moral life and political practice. The question of the use of political theory can thus be divided into two questions. First, What are the uses of the recommendations? Second, What are the uses of the philosophizing about political practice? (As we see in the next paragraph, the uses of philosophizing about moral life are inseparably joined to the uses of recommendations concerning political ends.) We shall leave aside the question of the use of the old books for those who wish to produce new political theories, or engage in any aspect of the larger enterprise of moral speculation about politics. Our subject is the use of the old books for political scientists whose main purpose is to study, not to recommend.

On the use of the recommendations, it must be said that the first benefit is moral guidance. To call moral guidance a benefit, one must assume that all men absorbed by politics, as actors, students, or curious bystanders, stand in need of instruction on how to respond to, and make assessment of, the mad whirl of political phenomena. Most people approach politics with some preconceptions. But preconceptions are not sufficient fortification against the inevitable confusion. Political theories offer the working out of political positions with a thoroughness and determination beyond the patience or skill of all but a gifted few. If one wants to know what it means, all in all, to espouse the value of social peace at any price, to know what it costs, to know what may make it necessary to pay the cost, to know the kinds of argument men use to attack the value, to know the relation between social peace and other values, how could one do better than to read either St. Augustine or Hobbes? One may finally declare oneself an Augustinian or a Hobbesian, or one may not. If one does, the substantial beginnings of one's own position are found in a book. One is then free to revise their teachings or alter the mode of their derivation, or bring them up to date, or apply them to circumstances unknown to St. Augustine or Hobbes. In any case, one will find a ready-made argument. If one cannot accept their doctrines, one at least understands why someone is willing to cherish social peace above everything else. A careful articulation of a position invites criticism and makes it possible for a counterposition to be formulated.

Similarly, on the matter of governmental means, political theory offers the most elaborate *rationales*. Forms of government are not simply there, like a force of nature. They are open to considered acceptance or rejection, or to some compromise response. If one wants to know what is required to keep a system of representative government in being, what the condition of the population must be, how the system compares with other systems, what its dangers are, what moral and practical possibilities it stimulates and which ones it discourages, what its parts are and how the parts work with or inhibit each other, how could one do better than to read Mill's *Considerations on Representative Government*, or Tocqueville's *Democracy in America*? Neither writer had the last word, but once again, the substantial beginnings of argument are to be found in their work. Is it not right to say that moral guidance about both ends and means contributes to political knowledge? We must insist that political theory is not mere preference, but the defense of preference, which invariably lays on the writer the burden of lengthy, rational exposition. Such exposition must take facts, and classes of fact, into account and must discipline them. Systemic generalities abound. Models of political systems are offered for reflection. Naturally, knowledge will be forthcoming, along with the guidance. One may add that, guidance apart, the works of political theories are examples of moral and practical reasoning. They teach their readers how to construct moral arguments about political phenomena. They demonstrate the extent of the relevant, the amount of complex reality that must pass before the mind of anyone who wishes to be adequate to the trial of convincingly (or plausibly) saying why he prefers something to something else in politics.

The Uses of Philosophizing about Practice

On the uses of philosophizing, far less apology is called for. As we have already said, a great deal of American political science is occupied with definitions of the political, with conceptual analysis, with the search for keys and metaphors, with the enumeration of the elements of any politics, with classification, with asking the right questions, with placing the political in the context of culture. All these things fill the pages of political theory. To define the political, one surely must start with Locke's definition in the *Second Treatise*. To explicate the concept of freedom, one surely must start with Hobbes's analysis in the *Leviathan*. To explicate the concept of justice, one surely must start with the first two books of *The Republic*.

One could go on to praise Aristotle for his view of the elements of politics, and Plato, Aquinas, Machiavelli, Hobbes, Montesquieu, Hegel, Bentham, and others for their effort to find the key to politics, and to suggest a metaphor, an imaginative abridgement, for the essence of politics. The work of these men is not ended: it can never be finished and done with. But we cannot overlook their work; we cannot afford to waste their ardor. A partisan of political theory must resist the temptation to say, "It's all in Aristotle" (or Hobbes or Locke). "It" could not possibly be in the writings of one man, or one tradition. Emerson's rebuke is healthy:

> The longest wave is quickly lost in the sea. Plato would willingly have a Platonism, a known and accurate expression for the world, and it should be accurate. It shall be the world passed through the mind of Plato—nothing less. . . . He has clapped copyright on the world. . . . But the mouthful proves too large. *Boa constrictor* has good will to eat it, but he is foiled. He falls abroad in the attempt, and biting, gets strangled: the bitten world holds the biter fast by his own teeth. There he perishes: unconquered nature lives on and forgets him. So it fares with all: so must it fare with Plato. . . . These things we are forced to say if we must consider the effort of Plato or of any philosopher to dispose of nature—which will not be disposed of.[8]

These things we too are forced to say about any political theorist in regard to the world of politics. Having said that, however, we can still praise political theorists for their *hubris*. In their pride we learn.

But the famous political theories are greater than their recommendations and their *formal* philosophizing. Ultimately, their greatness derives from the fact that they are displays of *sensibility*. Where else than to Plato should one go to find an expression of the political mind when it is world-hating and austere; than to Aristotle, when it is worldly and in love with the inexhaustible richness of politics; than to Cicero, when it is awed by the majesty of politics; than to St. Augustine, when it is sickened by the horror of politics; than to Aquinas, when it seeks to balance piety with concessions to human frailty; than to Machiavelli, when it contemplates politics under the aspect of agonistic exertion; than to Hobbes, when it loves and hates the irrational absurdities of political motives; than to Locke, when it makes the demand for decency absolute; than to Montesquieu, when it tries to determine the limits of the politically possible; than to Rousseau, when it imposes on politics the necessity to square with the most basic and most radical moral expectations; than to Burke, when it manages to color conservative practice with the most beautiful coloring; than to Paine, when it drops caution in order to risk the most amazing simplicities; than to Hegel, when it wrestles to force every kind of human fact into a political mold; than to Mill, when it is most liberally infatuated with contrast and variety? Political theory is not

---

[8] Ralph Waldo Emerson, "Plato; or The Philosopher," in *Representative Men* (Boston: Houghton Mifflin, 1884), pp. 75–77.

cumulative; it does not add up to a single theory. Instead it is made up of the best concentrations of sensibility—not blueprints, not "isms," not answers or solutions. They are permanently useful, because there is, through all mutations, continuity in human predicament.

And sensibility is expressed in figurative and inventive utterance, in observations, in persuasive definitions, in asides, in scattered passages. There is a quality of intellectual excess in all the great political theories. There is a power of suggestiveness that explains the addiction of scholars to them, the constant need to reread and interpret them, that gives a warrant to commentators to spin out their successive versions of, say, Plato or Hobbes or Burke. There is more in them than a student can use profitably on any given occasion. They change before our eyes, as all great works of literary style and imaginative conception do. The parts are greater than the whole; the meanings extracted are greater than the meaning intended. From these expressions of the political mind—the best we have—men can, if they have a will to do so, receive hints and clues that enable them to engage in all the operations of the political scientist, from the humble one of meeting the demands of the layman, to providing detailed descriptions, to framing hypotheses, to knowing what sorts of systemic generality matter, to philosophizing about practice, and, most grandly, to pondering such generalities of wisdom as we are fortunate enough to know and letting them sink into our own political sensibilities throughout a lifetime of political study.

Bibliography

The following articles, parts of books, and books contain valuable writing on both the nature and uses of political theory.

Benn, Stanley I., "Nature of Political Philosophy" in *The Encyclopedia of Philosophy*. 8 vols. New York: Macmillan, 1967. Vol. 6, pp. 387-392.

Berlin, Isaiah, "Does Political Theory Still Exist?" in Peter Laslett and W. G. Runciman (eds.), *Philosophy, Politics and Society* (Second Series). Oxford: Basil Blackwell, 1962.

Bluhm, William T., *Theories of the Political System*. Englewood Cliffs, N.J.: Prentice-Hall, 1965. Chaps. I and XV.

Brecht, Arnold, *Political Theory*. Princeton: Princeton University Press, 1959.

Catlin, George, "Political Theory: What Is It?" *Political Science Quarterly*, LXXII (No. 1), 1957, pp. 1-29.

Chapman, John W., "Political Theory: Logical Structure and Enduring Types," *Annales de philosophie politique*, VI, 1965, pp. 57-96.

Cobban, Alfred, "The Decline of Political Theory," *Political Science Quarterly*, LXVII (No. 3), 1953, pp. 321-337.

Easton, David, *The Political System*. New York: Alfred A. Knopf, 1953. Chaps. IX-XII.

Eckstein, Harry, "Political Theory and the Study of Politics: A Report of a Conference," *The American Political Science Review*, L (No. 2), 1956, pp. 475-487.

Germino, Dante, "The Revival of Political Theory," *The Journal of Politics*, XXV (No. 3), 1963, pp. 437-460.

Gewirth, Alan, Introduction, *Political Philosophy*. New York: Macmillan, 1965.

Hacker, Andrew, *Political Theory*. New York: Macmillan, 1961. Chap. 1.

Hyneman, Charles S., *The Study of Politics*. Urbana: University of Illinois Press, 1959. Chap. XI.

Jenkin, Thomas P., *The Study of Political Theory*. New York: Doubleday, 1955.

de Jouvenel, Bertrand, *The Pure Theory of Politics*. Cambridge: Cambridge University Press, 1963. Chap. 3.

Macdonald, Margaret, "The Language of Political Theory" in A. G. N. Flew (ed.), *Logic and Language* (First Series). Oxford: Basil Blackwell, 1951.

McCloskey, H. J., "The Nature of Political Philosophy," *Ratio*, VI (No. 1), 1964, pp. 50-62.

Oakeshott, Michael, "The Study of 'Politics' in a University" in Michael Oakeshott, *Rationalism in Politics*. New York: Basic Books, 1962.

Olafson, Frederick A. (ed.), Introduction, *Society, Law, and Morality*. Englewood Cliffs, N.J.: Prentice-Hall, 1961.

Partridge, P. H., "Politics, Philosophy, Ideology," *Political Studies*, IX (No. 3), 1961, pp. 217-235.

Plamenatz, John, *Man and Society*. 2 vols. New York: McGraw-Hill Book Company, 1963. Introduction, vol. I.

Riemer, Neal, *The Revival of Democratic Theory*. New York: Appleton-Century-Crofts, 1962. Chap. 1.

Runciman, W. G., *Social Science and Political Theory*. Cambridge: Cambridge University Press, 1963. Chap. VIII.

Sabine, George H., "What Is a Political Theory?" *Journal of Politics*, I (No. 1), 1939, pp. 1-16.

Smith, David G., "Political Science and Political Theory," *The American Political Science Review*, LI (No. 3), 1957, pp. 734-746.

Strauss, Leo, "An Epilogue" in Herbert J. Storing (ed.), *Essays on the Scientific Study of Politics*. New York: Holt, Rinehart and Winston, 1962.

————, "Political Philosophy and History" and "What Is Political Philosophy?" in Leo Strauss, *What Is Political Philosophy?* Glencoe, Ill.: Free Press, 1959.

Wolin, Sheldon S., *Politics and Vision*. Boston: Little, Brown, 1960. Chap. 1.

Index